PELICAN

THE MEDIEV.

John B. Morrall, born in 1923, was educated at King Edward VI School, Birmingham, and at New College, Oxford. He has specialized in the study and teaching of medieval history and has held university teaching posts in this field in Dublin (University College) and London (the London School of Economics). He is now Senior Lecturer in Political Science at the London School of Economics. His publications include *Political Thought in Medieval Times*, *Gerson and the Great Schism*, *Church and State through the Centuries* (in collaboration with S. Z. Ehler) and a number of articles.

JOHN B. MORRALL

The Medieval Imprint

THE FOUNDING OF
THE WESTERN EUROPEAN
TRADITION

PENGUIN BOOKS

Penguin Books Ltd, Harmondsworth, Middlesex, England
Penguin Books Inc., 7110 Ambassador Road, Baltimore, Maryland 21207, U.S.A.
Penguin Books Australia Ltd, Ringwood, Victoria, Australia

—

First published by C. A. Watts 1967
Published in Pelican Books 1970

—

—

Made and printed in Great Britain
by C. Nicholls & Company Ltd
Set in Linotype Pilgrim

CONTENTS

PREFACE   7

ACKNOWLEDGEMENTS   9

1 INTRODUCTORY : THE DEBATE ON THE
  MIDDLE AGES   11

2 BUILDING ON THE RUINS OF ROME   30

3 THE DILEMMAS OF MEDIEVAL
  CHRISTIANITY   52

4 LORDS, LADIES, LAND AND PEOPLE   98

5 TOWNS, TRADE, TECHNOLOGY AND
  THOUGHT   135

6 EPILOGUE: MEDIEVAL GOVERNMENT AND
  ITS DILEMMA   156

SELECT BIBLIOGRAPHY   165

INDEX   169

PREFACE

AN imprint of any kind has a twofold character. On the one hand it is a lingering symbol of an event or process now in the past; on the other hand its continuing and visible existence here and now cannot avoid having an effect on the happenings of the present. It is in a sense both dead and alive. This is what the author believes to be true of the Middle Ages and this is why this book has received its present title. In particular it will be contended that the Middle Ages saw the birth of an essential feature of Western civilization – the concept of the person as the unit of social 'discourse'. This concept, the author holds, differentiates Western culture from all others and is the chief bond of continuity between the 'medieval' and 'modern' periods. It was the growing tension caused by the articulation of this personalist concept into more rigid though perhaps inevitable institutional forms which led to the decline of medieval society in the fourteenth and fifteenth centuries and the rise of new themes in the social pattern, a twin process which forms the real distinction between 'medieval' and 'modern'. There is no abrupt break; the historical tension and the historian's distinction alike are, it may be suggested, to be traced back to the efforts of the Western European 'personalist' ideal to find ever more adequate modes of expression.

In a book of this size it would obviously be impossible to attempt a detailed study of every aspect of European medieval culture; the author has therefore contented himself with laying emphasis on motifs illustrating his main theme as enunciated in the introductory chapter. This is what appears to him to be the most intellectually satisfying way of interpreting the medieval period and of indicating its connexion with our own. He is aware that the same evidence might be interpreted in widely different ways, which might appear to the reader to be equally, if not more, valid. He will be glad if, at least, the views he puts forward stimulate further discussion, and he will in this connexion echo the words of Burckhardt (more modest in sustaining his own thesis than most of his disciples):

To each age, perhaps, the outlines of a given civilization present a different picture; and in treating of a civilization which is the mother of our own, and whose influence is still at work among us, it is unavoidable that individual judgement and feeling should tell every moment both on the writer and on the reader. In the wide ocean upon which we venture, the possible ways and directions are many; and the same studies which have served for this work might easily in other hands not only receive a wholly different treatment and application, but lead also to essentially different conclusions. Such indeed is the importance of the subject that it still calls for fresh investigation, and may be studied with advantage from the most varied points of view. Meanwhile we are content if a patient hearing is granted us, and if this book be taken and judged as a whole.[1]

1. *The Civilization of the Renaissance in Italy*, translation by S. G. C. Middlemore, Phaidon Press edition, 1944, p. 1.

ACKNOWLEDGEMENTS

I WOULD like to express particular thanks to my wife who, by her suggestion of the title for this book, found for me a succinct expression of what I believe to be the relationship between the medieval and modern European cultures. I have in fact profited over a long period and to no small extent from wide-ranging discussion with her on all manner of topics directly or indirectly relevant to the book.

The idea of my writing this book was first suggested to me by Mr T. M. Schuller. At times, when more aware than usual of my own presumption in tackling such a huge subject in so small a compass, I have wondered if I really ought to feel grateful to him! But at all stages the book has benefited from his considered and painstaking advice.

J. B. M.

London, December, 1966

INTRODUCTORY: THE DEBATE ON
THE MIDDLE AGES

EVERY student of history has to come to grips, sooner or later, with the problem of periodization. The division of past human experience into a number of rationally distinguishable stages is more than a handy device for use in examination syllabuses or academic textbooks; it is essential for even the most rudimentary assessment of public as well as private life. Any individual looking back on his own career can appreciate divisions within it, not only those obvious ones shared with others, such as the progress from childhood into maturity, and on to old age, but also stages peculiar to himself – the change to a new job at a particular time, successful or unsuccessful love affairs, conversions to deeply felt religious or political beliefs, expected or unexpected strokes of good or bad luck, and so on. The same applies in the lives of nations and societies, on a naturally larger scale – here, too, economic changes, new directions of social attraction or social discontent, the impact of religious and political gospels, the catastrophes of climate, warfare or disease play their part. The Greek philosopher Heraclitus was tempted to write off any rational explanation of these divisions by asserting, 'All things are in a state of change,' and leaving it at that; Sean O'Casey's remark, 'The whole world is in a terrible state of chassis,' embodies much the same outlook. But for most of those interested in looking back on the lives of their societies or at least themselves, the matter cannot rest there; the common complaint, 'I do not see why this should have happened to me,' is an instinctive refusal to accept an apparently purposeless pattern in past events. The pursuit for an explanation is in the end found to be inescapable.

This general and usually unformulated common human impulse is possessed in an acutely developed degree by those interested in the study of history. As far as the writer of history is concerned, the impulse shows itself in two possible approaches, corresponding respectively to what we may call the 'how' and the 'why' of historical events. Historians interested primarily in the 'how' of the past will be more likely to choose a particular segment of history and investigate the various assessable factors (economic, political, philosophical and the like) which they consider to have any bearing on the event or events which they are trying to explain. The 'why' approach, on the other hand, will aim at establishing necessary causal connexions between historical events and epochs, even between *all* historical events and epochs, and so will end by constructing a 'philosophy of history', as did Augustine, Bossuet or Hegel.

Of recent years the 'hows' have tended to be dominant and a considerable amount of distrust has been lavished on the 'whys'. Yet there is nothing necessarily incompatible between the two approaches, provided each is careful not to trespass on the other's ground. One and the same historian may be able to establish what he thinks to be the truest and fullest assessable factors of a given period of history, and at the same time feel able to suggest why things happened in such and such an overall pattern. In fact, when one analyses the matter further, assertions which can possess meaning only when seen as part of an implicit philosophy of history can easily be found in the works of the most pragmatic of historians.

Both approaches are impossible without some sort of system of periodization. Some of these systems are more obvious than others; a writer of a history of the First or Second World War, for instance, would be confronted with a clearly defined period of military hostilities, with a rather less clearly defined area of causes (remote and proximate) and side and after effects. If Bossuet, Hegel or Augustine had been writing about either or both of the wars, they would also have felt the necessity of fitting the history they were unravelling into their general philosophy of the history of mankind.

With a concept such as 'the Middle Ages' the case is far different. There are no certain chronological limits to act as guides. The very phrase itself begs a large number of questions. What are we to understand, for example, by 'middle'? A chronologically central point or a position of logical or cultural centrality? In either case the standard of reference by which to judge will obviously change with the passage of time. And so in fact the term 'Middle Ages' has been subject to as many different uses or abuses as the twin term 'Renaissance' with which it has so often been antithetically associated. The present chapter will try to trace some of the past presentations of the concept and we shall see that throughout its metamorphosis the two ways of approaching history, the 'how' and the 'why', have both played their part.

The German Protestant seventeenth-century annalist Cellarius seems to have been the first writer to use the term 'Middle Age' in its now familiar chronological sense, but the term as well as the concept symbolized by the term is considerably older in origin.

'We shall see,' declares Cellarius, 'that a more efficient arrangement will be achieved, if we take ancient history as going as far as Constantine the Great, the history of the Middle Age (*medii aevi*) to the Fall of Constantinople, and finally modern history (*novam*) to our own times.' The sense of symmetry may be suspected in Cellarius' decision to take the rise of Constantine on the one hand and the fall of the capital Constantine founded on the other as his two points of division. But his division stuck, though the dividing lines he had enunciated were often and variously modified. In point of fact Cellarius was merely crystallizing a periodization which had been in process of formulation for two hundred years before and which owed its initial impetus to factors not primarily connected with the disinterested study of history.

From about the beginning of the fifteenth to the middle of the sixteenth century the main feature of the intellectual and cultural horizon is a feeling of revolt and reaction against the whole development of the previous thousand years. In the cultural sphere this takes the form of an attempt, real or spurious according to one's opinion, to recover the essence of classical Roman and Greek tradition. In the religious sphere there is a parallel appeal back to the example and authority of the uncorrupted primitive Church. In each case the long stretch of time between the fall of Rome and the contemporary age itself comes to be regarded as an irksome, useless and even wicked intermediate gap, historically pointless and intellectually, culturally and spiritually barren. Matteo Palmieri, writing in the mid 1430s complains: 'The real guides to distinction in all the arts, the solid foundation of all civilization, have been lost to mankind for eight hundred years and more.

It is but in our own day that men dare boast that they see the dawn of better things.'[1] Here we have the germ of the concept of 'the Middle Ages', which Palmieri implicitly equates with what later became another familiar periodizing concept, 'the Dark Ages'.

It may be noted, however, that the Humanists seem to differ widely among themselves about when precisely the benighted middle period ended. Writing a century after Palmieri, Vasari, in his famous *Lives of the Artists* (written, one wonders, as a contrast and a counterblast to the medieval *Lives of the Saints*) pushes back the beginning of artistic revival well into the thirteenth century. 'In 1250 heaven took pity on the talented men who were being born in Tuscany and led them back to the pristine forms.'[2] The religious and almost Messianic tinge of Vasari's language is worth notice; clearly the concept of cultural renovation was still closely linked with that of religious renewal, both being equally due to Divine initiative rather than autonomous historical factors.

As might be expected, the same conceptual pattern may be traced in the attitude of the Protestant Reformers to the Catholic centuries which lay between them and their idolized primitive Church.

Even before the Reformation similar ideas had been current in less orthodox discussions of the history of the Church. Heretical and semi-orthodox religious movements, such as the Joachites, had spoken of three periods of revelation, corresponding to the Persons of the Trinity – the age of the Father being the Old Testament period, the age of the Son being linked, obviously

1. Translation by W. A. Woodward, *Studies in Education During the Age of the Renaissance*.
2. Vasari, *Lives of the Artists*, translation by G. Bull, Penguin Classics, p. 45.

enough, to the development of the Christian Church
after Christ, while the final and most perfect period, the
reign of the Holy Ghost, had been scheduled by the
Joachites to begin in the thirteenth century. The Church
of the thirteenth century paid more attention than we
need do to these lucubrations; all we need note is that in
them we once more find the notion of a period of im-
perfect and intermediate development, though the
Joachites did not go as far as to declare this intermediate era as positively evil.

It was left for Luther, following (as he did in many
respects) the ideas previously sketched by John Huss, to
take this further step. For Luther the period following
the death of Pope Gregory the Great (604) was a grim
age in which no less a figure than Antichrist himself had
succeeded in getting possession of the visible machin-
ery of the Church through control of a corrupt Papacy.
The challenge to the Roman Church which Luther con-
ceived himself as making in his own time heralded the
end of the intermediate age of Antichrist's domination,
and it is interesting to note that Luther's periodization
affords another instance of a division of history which
regards what we now term 'the Middle Ages' as a unified field of consideration. It is of only secondary con-
cern for our particular purposes, though not for those
of Luther himself, that the Reformer in point of fact
thought that the new age which he was inaugurating
would be the herald, not of 'modern times', but of the
end of the world.

This sense of a new age which had revived primitive
Christian purity of religion after an intermediate period
of corruption became a characteristic of Protestant historiography (its most massive specimen being Flacius
Illyricus' *Centuries of Magdeburg*) and was crystallized
after the permanent division of the Churches from the

middle of the sixteenth century onwards. By the middle
seventeenth century we find Milton talking of the Reformation as already a definite event in the past and
chiding his more episcopally minded fellow country-
men for not having carried it to its logical conclusion
('our four-score years vexation of Him (God) in this
our wildernesse since Reformation began').[3]

Already, then, we find 'the Middle Ages' cast for
what was to be its accustomed role of unwelcome de-
layer of both cultural 'Renaissance' and religious 'Reformation'. In Catholic countries the 'Reformation'
periodization would naturally not be used for the same
purpose; it is true that one finds some Catholic writers
looking back with nostalgia to the days before the religious split of Christendom, and to this extent they too
would add to the tendency to separate 'medieval' and
'modern' periods. Cardinal Baronius, for example, in
his *Annales Ecclesiastici* (1588–1607) is concerned to
establish the notion of the medieval Papacy as an un-
questioned social and political as well as theological
guide to Christendom. So was born the perennial concept, adopted down to the present by many Catholic and
non-Catholic writers alike, of the Middle Ages as 'the
Ages of Faith'. On the whole, however, Catholic writers emphasized, for obvious apologetic purposes, the
historical continuity reaching back from their own age
to the early Christian period. Bossuet, for instance, pre-
fers to make a political rather than religious dividing
line and uses Charlemagne's coronation in 800 to make
a rather utilitarian dichotomy in his account of universal history. Paradoxically it was the anti-Catholic
thinkers of the Continental Enlightenment who crystallized the concept of the Middle Ages as a working

3. *Animadversions upon The Remonstrants*, Works of John
Milton, Nonesuch edition, p. 544.

hypothesis to back up their own onslaught on the established Catholicism of their own time.

   The attitude of the Enlightenment publicists in France
and elsewhere was coloured by their view of the Catholic institutional Christianity of their own time as the
lineal successor to the Church of the Middle Ages. For
Voltaire the medieval period was either to be treated
with contempt or dismissed with obloquy in the same
manner as *l'infame* of his own time. For Gibbon the
fall of the Roman Empire was due to 'the triumph of
barbarism and Christianity', while Alexander Pope,
with his usual poetic neatness, summed up the now
familiar 'Renaissance and Reformation' versus 'Middle
Ages' antithesis in some lines from his *Essay on Criticism* –

> Learning and Rome alike in Empire grew,
>   And Arts still follow'd where her eagles flew;
> From the same foes, at last, both felt their doom,
> And the same age saw learning fall, and Rome.
> With tyranny, then superstition join'd,
> As that the body, this enslav'd the mind;
> Much was believ'd, but little understood,
> And to be dull was constru'd to be good;
> A second deluge learning thus o'er-run,
> And the monks finished what the Goths begun.
> At length, Erasmus, that great injur'd name,
> (The glory of the priesthood, and the shame!)
> Stemm'd the wild torrent of a barb'rous age,
> And drove those holy Vandals off the stage.
> But see! each Muse, in Leo's golden days,
> Starts from her trance, and trims her wither'd bays!
> Rome's ancient genius, o'er its ruins spread,
> Shakes off the dust, and rears his rev'rend head![4]

   A more favourable version of the distinction between
'medieval' and 'modern' was given by intellectual and

4. Pope, *An Essay on Criticism*, 1. 683-700.

political elements in Western European countries
which had become disturbed or frightened by the expansion of monarchical central power. In the France of
the sixteenth-century wars of religion the medieval
period was looked back to by the publicists like F. Hot-
man as the age of uncorrupted constitutionalism in
contrast with the contemporary trend towards despot-
ism. Publicists of the Stuart period in England followed
the same line with greater emphasis – parliamentary
lawyers such as Coke appealed to historical precedents
as a weapon against the encroachments of the King and
the myth of Magna Carta was born. The more extreme
English seventeenth-century radicals were more antiquarian still; for the Levellers nothing after 1066 and
violated Anglo-Saxon custom could claim any respect.
On a more sober level, quieter scholars on both sides began to embark on serious historical investigation of the
medieval origins of their own modern institutions and
social practices. The work of most of them was indeed
usually actuated by the desire to prove a partisan case.
Thus the pioneering investigations of Sir Henry Spelman into the feudal system were motivated by a Royal-
ist wish to show that all legal privileges emanated from
the King. Harrington's only slightly disguised 'fictional'
account of English historical development in *Oceana* is
aimed at demonstrating that a balanced distribution of
property, particularly landed property, is essential for a
true 'commonwealth' such as he supposed Oliver Cromwell was engaged in establishing. With all their respective
biases, such studies as those of Spelman and Harrington
focused attention on medieval legal and economic
development as possessing its own intrinsic importance,
and their interpretations of it are by no means completely
superseded even at the present time.

In the field of ecclesiastical history the French Benedictines of St Maur had set medieval studies on a new path by insisting on the necessity of first-hand establishment of the authenticity of sources by scientific methods. At about the same time as Richard Simon, the Oratorian, was laying the foundations of modern Biblical criticism, Mabillon and his Benedictine confreres were creating the scientific disciplines of diplomacy and palaeography, indispensable for the direct study of medieval written sources. In the following century, Muratori's great collection of critically edited Italian medieval sources was to prove how the new scientific method could be applied to secular history.

An equally scholarly approach to medieval topics is to be found in the work of the great legal historians, such as the sixteenth-century Cujas. Cujas, reacting against the medieval attempt to retain a practical universal validity for Roman Law, insisted on studying that law as a purely historical phenomenon and made a point of refusing to treat it in terms of its contemporary relevance. At once more antiquarian and less utilitarian than his medieval predecessors, Cujas provides one more instance of the identification and definition of 'the Middle Ages' by means of self-conscious opposition to one or more of its leading ideas. For all its historical detachment, the school of Cujas was embarking on a deliberate path of departure from 'medieval' concepts.

The same may be said of those writers, such as Francis Bacon in England and la Popelinière in France, who helped to disseminate the notion of the superiority of 'modern' over 'ancient' learning, meaning by 'ancient' the thought-world of the Greek and Latin classics. The conflict, immortalized for English readers in Swift's *Battle of the Books*, was primarily a revolution of the supporters of a brave new world, such as Bacon, against the older Renaissance humanistic tradition for which human wisdom lay in faithful adherence to the unsurpassed Graeco-Roman models. The advocates of the 'moderns' had no direct interest in rehabilitating or even discussing the Middle Ages; yet the questioning of earlier humanism's axiom of the classical world as an absolute norm for historical judgement of civilization did indirectly pave the way for a more genuine appreciation of the Middle Ages as something more than a hiatus.

It was left for the fathers of modern sociology and history to go further still and claim that the Middle Ages was not only a fact, but a necessary fact. Vico's *New Science* is a bewildering mixture of blind alleys with pregnant insights; but one of his most influential concepts from a historiographical point of view is his contention that every civilization must pass through a cycle of 'divine', 'heroic' and 'human' ages, forming as Vico puts it 'the eternal history of humanity'. To the 'divine' or ritualistically dominated ages of early antiquity, corresponded for Vico the earlier European Middle Ages. The 'heroic' aristocratically dominated age of Roman development was exactly repeated in medieval feudalism, while the 'human' or rational development of the classical world under the Empire was paralleled, argued Vico (a convinced monarchist), by the efflorescence of modern culture under the enlightened despots of his own day. The Middle Ages thus acquired respectability as an integral, though not final, phase of the European exemplar of a law of universal historical development, but it did so at the price which must be paid by all exemplars – the risk of losing its own special identity. In this case specific appreciation of the medieval age in Western Europe was lost in the general and cloudy Viconian concept of a necessarily 'medieval' or 'feudal' phase of *every* civilized society. This particular heritage of Vico has had a remarkable life-span and is by no means dead even yet, as witness the title of an ambitious recent volume, *Feudalism in History*,[5] which attempts a comparative study of 'feudal' features in the Ancient East, China, India, Japan, Byzantium and elsewhere.

The Romantic school of historiography, which included historians both sympathetic and antipathetic to the Middle Ages, did at any rate provide an antidote to Vico's abstractionism by anchoring the study of the European Middle Ages firmly where it always should be anchored – in the evidence provided by European history itself. Most of the Romantics ran no danger of viewing European developments as no more than a symbol of a necessary universal historical process; indeed, many of them, such as Michelet, wrote from an intensely, even narrowly nationalistic viewpoint. Particularly among German writers, the 'Gothic centuries' embodied the most colourful and characteristic ages of their nation's heroic past. Hegel took this tendency to its extreme by standing universalism, so to speak, on its head when he made world history symbolical of European rather than the reverse. His justification was that only in Europe, according to him, had man's genius become capable of attaining its full development. For Hegel the Middle Ages, as he describes it in that strange book, *The Phenomenology of Mind*, was the period when man (that is to say all that mattered to him, *European man*) was passing through the phase of 'Spirit in self-estrangement', that is he had not yet attained a full and rationally free knowledge of himself. Without being caught up in Hegel's terminological jungle, it is worth noting that he views the period from the Fall of

5. *Feudalism in History*, ed. R. Coulborn.

Rome to the French Revolution as a single connected whole, what Tocqueville later was to call the *ancien régime*. This idea would, if it had been generally accepted, have tended to break down the distinction between 'medieval' and 'modern' or at any rate to make the chronological point of distinction nearly contemporary.

On the whole, however, it was not accepted. The stronger intellectual current of the time was still inclined to think of the Renaissance–Reformation period as the great watershed of change in the European past. Catholic reactionaries like Joseph de Maistre regarded the Protestant spirit as the direct ancestor of the French Revolutionary mind, while sober historians like Ranke saw the same period as the point of origin of the nation State, which to them was the most significantly distinctive feature of modern history. The perfection of the technique and methodology of scientific historical study also tended to isolate and emphasize the uniqueness of the past, including the medieval past, rather than its continuity with the present.

But the biggest factor in encouraging the drawing of hard and fast lines between 'medieval' and 'modern' was undoubtedly the mental climate produced by the Industrial Revolution, and it is no accident that it was in Western countries like Britain, France, Belgium, Western Germany and Switzerland, where the new economic changes went furthest, that 'the Middle Ages' as an historical period began to be most sharply differentiated. The general problem of the influence of social change on historiographical interests and attitudes is an almost virgin field of study; but the approach of the historical intelligentsia of the nineteenth century to the medieval period would provide a magnificent case history for such an investigation. Broadly speaking, it can be said that Western historians of the nineteenth century were above all impressed with the contrast between their own age of vast technological, social and hence intellectual upheaval on the one hand and previous ages of apparently more stable and static society on the other. The obsessive quest of such historians became the search for the roots of these changes which had, as they rightly thought, metamorphosed the Western European world. And the factors above all which most of them agreed had acted as catalysts for the changes were Nationalism, Rationalism and economic private enterprise, soon to be christened 'Capitalism'. And it began to be more and more accepted as the consensus of historical opinion that the fifteenth and sixteenth centuries formed the decisive period which saw the rising of these mighty forces and the mental outlook accompanying them. This entailed the corollary that an immense mental gulf separated the medieval from the modern world.

It is true that interpretation of the details of this consensue varied very widely. Cobbett's *History of the Reformation*, though written by a stout Protestant, is almost Chestertonian in its idealization of 'merrie' medieval England, while novelists like Scott and (with more reservations) Hugo also feel the attraction of the medieval past. Bishop Stubbs seeks painstakingly in medieval England for the adumbrations of the Victorian Constitution which he feels must surely be there, while for Freeman, as for the Levellers, everything worth while in English culture fell with Harold at Hastings. Chateaubriand reveres the Middle Ages as the age of Christian unity before the great apostasy, while at the other end of the century G. G. Coulton is equally certain that the whole medieval period was an immense delaying action by the forces of bigotry and repression.

A striking feature of the nineteenth-century 'consensus' was the manner in which its presuppositions were accepted by leading thinkers from totally opposing forces of the political background. No one could have been more of a conservative than Jacob Burckhardt. At once fascinated and repelled by the rise of the democratic society of his time, Burckhardt's massive erudition was devoted to establishing the origins of the forces behind that society. In his most famous book, *The Civilization of the Renaissance in Italy*, he believed that he had done so. The titles of some of his chapters, 'The State as a Work of Art', 'The Discovery of the World and of Man', are indicative of his argument that in this period and area all that is characteristic of the modern European mind took its origin. For upwards of one hundred years Burckhardt's interpretation was accepted as authoritative and with it the implied conclusion that 'medieval' and 'modern' were different, not only in degree, but in kind.

The outlook of Burckhardt, the nostalgically aristocratic conservative, was on this point paralleled by otherwise completely antagonistic thinkers of early Socialism. Saint-Simon admired the Middle Ages because he held that, by contrast with modern times, they had provided a unified spiritual ideology. In *The New Christianity* (1825) Saint-Simon contrasts, as illustration of his thesis, medieval Catholicism and degenerate 'post-Leo X' Catholicism. Once again the sixteenth century provides the crucial watershed. Nearly a century after Saint-Simon Prince Peter Kropotkin, at the other end of the Socialist spectrum, saw the fifteenth and sixteenth centuries as marking the beginning of 'the State period', when the 'mutual aid' of autonomous cities and corporations was crushed by what Kropotkin, as a good Anarchist, saw as the illegitimate pressure of public sovereign power.

But the most impressive witness for this nearly universal Socialist attitude to the Middle Ages is undoubtedly Marx himself. For him the difference between medieval and modern times was synonymous with the difference between feudal and capitalist society, each of these being themselves part of an inevitable historical development. The *Communist Manifesto* puts the process, as Marxism saw it, in a nutshell:

From the serfs of the Middle Ages sprang the chartered burghers of the earliest towns. From these burgesses the first elements of the *bourgeoisie* developed.

The discovery of America, the rounding of the Cape, opened up fresh ground for the rising *bourgeoisie*. The East India and Chinese markets, the colonization of America, trade with the colonies, the increase in the means of exchange and in commodities generally, gave to commerce, to navigation, to industry, an impulse never before known, and thereby, to the revolutionary element in the tottering feudal society, a rapid development.[6]

Sometimes Marx permits himself to view this process of the 'killing' of medieval social conditions by capitalism with some nostalgia: 'The *bourgeoisie*, wherever it has got the upper hand, has put an end to all feudal, patriarchal, idyllic relations.'[7] Elsewhere, however, this half-respect for feudalism is erased by what is almost a paean of praise for the world-encompassing success of capitalism. In both moods Marx was very close to adoring what he professedly wished to burn. But we are fortunately not committed here to analysis of the psychology of writers on economics and economic history.[8]

6. *Communist Manifesto*, I.   7. ibid.
8. This has actually been attempted by W. A. Weisshopf, *The Psychology of Economics* (1955), though with far from convincing results.

All that need be dwelt upon is the remarkable degree to which Marx's view of the economic significance of the Renaissance was accepted by friends and opponents alike. As late as 1932 we find Alfred von Martin writing in his *Sociology of the Renaissance* (still the only attempt at a synthesis of this subject):

'. . . the State itself was now becoming a capitalist entrepreneur; the politicians began to calculate and politics were becoming rational. Political decisions were influenced by commercial motives, and politics were closely circumscribed by the categories of means and ends dictated by bourgeoisie aims and interests. We see politics pervaded by the spirit of reason, which had been alien to the medieval State at a time when the Church had been the one rationally guided institution.'[9]

The famous identification of Protestant ethics with 'the spirit of capitalism' by Max Weber and his school was another variant on Marx's delimitation of the sixteenth century as the economic Great Divide. Historians of art and literature also tended to follow the theory of a sharp distinction between the medieval and modern ages and this theory still holds the field in most textbooks as well as in the popular mind.

Round about the period between the First and Second World Wars there were signs of a gathering reaction against this almost canonized interpretation. Increased study of the Middle Ages in many fields suggested that contrasts between that period and the Renaissance were by no means as sharp as Burckhardt had believed, and, though 'the problem of the Renaissance' is still hotly debated, the general verdict of scholarly opinion would now be against seeing the Renaissance as the massive dividing line it had previously been represented to be. This pushing back of the dividing line between Medieval

9. pp. 10-11, English translation, New York, 1963.

and Renaissance has even led some contemporary scholars to doubt the usefulness of the traditional categories at all; thus Armando Sapori argues that the real 'Renaissance' in all aspects of social life in Western Europe took place from the eleventh century onwards, and maintains that the period of stagnation between the fall of Rome and the eleventh-century revival might better possess the title of 'Middle Ages'. An American scholar, W. C. Bark, has gone even further and suggests that the period of revival is to be connected with the fall of the Roman Empire before the ultimately more progressive forces of Germanic barbarism and Christianity (an interesting reversal of Gibbon's position).

In the study of political ideas, too, the tendency of recent investigation has been to push back chronologically ideas such as State sovereignty and national feeling previously assumed to be characteristically Renaissance products. The title of a recent article by Gaines Post, one of the ablest of scholarly 'revisionists', is itself a deliberate and explicit challenge to Burckhardt.[10] A particularly interesting feature of recent research has been the demonstration of a hitherto unemphasized momentum of technological changes in the medieval period; some writers have seen in this the seeds of the European technological revolution which has so transformed world history.

Every writer on a controversial subject has an obligation to make his own position clear. The present author considers that the dichotomy between 'medieval' and 'modern' is no longer self-evidently valid; he hopes to present proof of this in the course of the book. At the same time he realizes that it is no use denying the pre-

10. 'Law and Politics in the Middle Ages: The Medieval State as a Work of Art', in *Perspectives in Medieval History* (Ed. K. F. Drew and F. S. Lear).

sence of a certain sense of 'otherness' felt by every modern when he considers the Middle Ages; the extreme advocates of continuity confuse the issue when they ignore this obvious fact. What the twentieth-century historian of the medieval period has to try to do is to account for this 'otherness' without recourse to unsubstantiated theories of cataclysmic break.

This is a very difficult task, just as difficult as it would be to work out an exact definition of the relationships between any given man and his father. The life-span of each coincides over a longer or shorter period of time; yet each enjoys or suffers sectors of experience which the other cannot share. The past hereditary and direct personal influence of the father may, even after his death, determine the son's behaviour in all sorts of incalculable ways. Conversely, the father's own paternal status carries his life into pathways which otherwise it would not have known. The father's life continues after the birth of the son; the son's life after the death of the father. In each there is change but not radical discontinuity. The analogy may serve as some explanation of the most fruitful way in which we may assess the relationship of 'medieval' to 'modern'. It is on this assumption that the argument of this work will proceed.

BUILDING ON THE RUINS
OF ROME

WHATEVER the variety of opinions about the chronological limits of the Middle Ages, there would be a
broad consensus about the most obvious social features
of the period. Firstly, it would be accepted that the
spiritual, intellectual and emotive life of the thousand
years between Rome and the Renaissance was conducted within the framework of ideas and problems
presented by the Christian religion in its Latin Catholic
form. Secondly, one could hardly question that a
landlord-tenant agricultural relationship became and remained the principal nexus of economic development
during the whole period, though this was supplemented,
not superseded, by the growth of towns and trade in the
latter part of the medieval era. Thirdly, the personal
character of the political and social framework, mani-
fested most significantly in phenomena such as feudalism, would have to be admitted. Any satisfactory account of the fundamental attributes of the medieval
world would have to attempt to define the nature and
trace the origins of these three main elements.

Of the three, Catholic Christianity was perhaps the
most axiomatic for the medieval outlook. The conversion of Constantine marked a spectacular change of
direction for the Roman world, just as the formal
splintering of Western Christian unity in the sixteenth
century is the open registration of the transformation
of medieval Western Europe into the geographically

more immense and intellectually more variegated society of modern times. This is not to deny that the Reformation was a culmination as well as a revolution; but at the same time the abandonment of the struggle to preserve in visible form the spiritual unity of Western Christendom made clear that a new chapter in the history of European society was opening.

In similar, though less positive fashion we may see the weakening of our other two elements as signs of the same transformation. We could plausibly argue that the supersession of agriculture by a growingly urban and industrial economy marks another chasm between medieval and modern, though it is far from clear that this factor could be said to be in full operation in most areas of Western Europe before the nineteenth century. It could be maintained with a rather bigger proportion of controversy that from the sixteenth century onwards social relationships tended to change from systems based on personal ties to those based on common membership of impersonal corporate organizations of which the State is the most gigantic example. But in the end the collapse of allegiance to the spiritual focus of medieval society, orthodox Catholic Christianity, would seem to emerge as the most decisive sign of the terminal point of medieval society, and this is the sense in which it will be understood in this volume. We shall also assume for our present purposes that, looking in the other historical direction, any intelligible account of the origins of medieval society would lead us back to the age of Diocletian and Constantine (*c.* A.D. 300), though, as we shall see, we have to wait for the age of Charlemagne and his successors (*c.* 800–1000) before the major constituents of the medieval world-structure come into explicit formulation. Throughout the whole period the ghost of Rome (if indeed it ever really died) remains to haunt the development of the West.

There is more than one point of contact (after due regard has been paid to historical uniqueness) between the period of the later Western Roman Empire and our own. Both were ages of intellectual ferment and political and economic reconstruction following on a disastrous epoch of foreign and civil wars, economic retrogression and collapse and social disintegration. In both dynamic new views of life were challenging long-accepted traditional beliefs and practices, while both periods, too, were obsessed with the fear of a catastrophe which would put an end to civilization as they knew it.

It was the achievement of the third-century Emperors that they made sincere and intelligent attempts to find the reasons for the threatened collapse of the Roman order and went on to prescribe carefully thought out remedies to avert it. Who shall say that they lacked success? It is true that the Empire in the West received only a temporary reprieve, as the result of their labours, from the death sentence which eventually overtook it, but nevertheless the work of the later Emperors did in fact lay the foundations for many elements which were to play a part in forming the enduring structure of medieval Europe.

Even without exterior menaces, there were already formidable tensions in the Imperial structure when Diocletian, Constantine and their successors took stock of it. One of these, perhaps the most obvious, is the constant monetary devaluation and inflation which set in, despite the attempts of various Emperors to stop the rot, from the end of the second century onwards, and which by the end of the third had rendered the silver coinage of the Empire practically valueless, much as the mark was in Germany of the 1920s. Coupled with this went a growing and natural tendency towards barter economy (even Imperial officials of the time often insisted on being paid in kind rather than money) and an adverse balance of trade caused mainly by the draining off of specie due to luxury commerce with the Middle East and beyond. (China had its first contacts with Rome in the second century.) When Diocletian and Constantine took the situation in hand one of their main preoccupations was to ensure a stable gold coinage and for centuries what remained of European monetary economy was to owe its stability and power of exchange to the gold *solidus*. But the strengthening of gold had only a partially beneficial effect on the general economic situation. The majority of inhabitants of the Empire were not rich enough to be able to count on large resources of golden coinage and for them the spectre of economic hardship, if not ruin, was never far off.

The economically underprivileged classes were largely peasants, and this suggests another radical weakness in the Roman economic and social structure. Though classical Graeco-Roman civilization, like every other society before the Industrial Revolution, rested on a necessary agricultural base, its values, its way of life and its intellectual ideals were linked to the concept of the city State. Alexander the Great and his successors, and later Rome itself, had established what looked on the surface like vast territorial monarchies, but which on closer examination revealed itself to be a collection of cities, whose inhabitants were indeed politically impotent but who had received as price for their political surrender a mass of economic and social privileges. The deliberate policy of Augustus and his successors for two centuries (*c.* A.D. 1–200) was to rely for the support of the Empire on the wealthy upper and middle urban classes. Even for the nobles of the senatorial aristocracy, who remained an honorific and at times politically significant group in the Imperial structure, country life was a sideline recreation; the real sphere of their social activity was the town. Economic distribution and production were geared to the convenience of the urban population; even the poorest of the latter, with their doles, free food and entertainment were immeasurably better off than their counterparts in the countryside. Rome in particular acted as a gigantic parasite sucking into its unproductive entrails the economic effort of the provinces.

In A.D. 212 a much discussed decree of the Emperor Caracalla extended Roman citizenship to all freemen throughout the Empire. The motives for this apparently generous gesture are obscure; perhaps those cynics are right who suspect that a desire to widen the scope of taxation was the principal incentive. But in any case the measure came too late to re-create social cohesion, and the third century was to see a terrible punishment for the complacent city populations. The cataclysm was brought about by what amounted to a coalition of interests between army and peasantry, caused by the fact that by now the army was rapidly becoming predominantly composed of the provincial peasantry themselves.

This predominant fact of third-century Roman power politics was responsible for a fundamental shift of economic and in the end of constitutional balance. From the time of Septimius Severus (193–210) onwards the Emperors had perceived that their own survival depended on continued appeasement of the army at all costs. When any of them showed signs of forgetting this bread-and-butter fact, they were quickly reminded of it by deposition or death or both. But this enforced reliance of the Imperial authority on an army of peasants, largely provincial and non-Italian, meant the breach of the traditional alliance, created so carefully by Augustus and his successors, between the Empire, the senatorial aristocracy and the urban middle classes. It is dangerous, of course, to view, as for example the great Russian historian Rostovtzeff has done, the third-century Roman internal struggle too explicitly in terms of a class war; but nevertheless it does seem impossible to deny that a consistent pattern of attack on the privileges of nobility and towns by a semi-civilized peasant soldiery can be discerned. As the century went on, the Emperors themselves came to be recruited from this class, having risen to the top by way of successful army careers. With this background they could hardly be expected to devote serious attention to clipping the wings of the rapacious army and in the case of Maximian (235–8) we find Imperial authority going so far as to accelerate the process of urban liquidation.

Another factor which made the army a dissolvent of the traditional order was the increasing number of full-blooded barbarians in its ranks. The barbarian invasion of the Empire was in fact not a cataclysmic *Blitzkrieg* in its early stages, but a slow process of infiltration across the frontiers, more often than not connived at by the Imperial authorities themselves. The Germanic new-comers found fraternization with the 'Roman' provincials who formed the army fairly easy and a military career with the prospects of plunder, pensions and land, which it held open, was an obvious proposition for these warrior peasants from across the Rhine and the Danube. By the end of the century their presence in the 'Roman' forces was so much taken for granted that an Egyptian mother could talk of her son having 'gone to join the barbarians' when in fact she meant that he had become a recruit to the Roman Imperial Army.

The hammer-blows struck at the urban economic

structure in the third century are clear enough from archaeological evidence alone. The shrinkage in the size of town areas is evident on many sites throughout the Empire; in England the most striking example is the decline of Verulam, with the abandonment of its municipal theatre and many of its private houses; Roman London tells the same story. The building of town walls for the first time for several centuries bears witness to growing insecurity. But possibly the most significant fact of all is the desertion of the towns by the aristocracy who, unlike the urban commercial and trading classes, were able to get out before the going became too difficult. The 'villas' which became the basic unit of upper-class life from the third century onwards were the outward sign of the aristocratic 'back to the land' movement; they were large country estates with a more or less luxurious collection of dwellings as their nucleus, which served as living-quarters and protection for nobles, retainers and subordinate workers and slaves. Crudely fortified as time went on, it is tempting to see in them the beginning of one aspect of feudalism itself – the landed estate based on personal allegiance as a result of military and economic needs. Certainly it seems to be true that the aristocracy, debarred as a rule either by choice or Imperial pressure from participation in the Imperial army, turned to organize their own military protection by means of unofficial private armies.

The unfortunate middle classes who were left in the towns felt the full weight of Imperial taxation and regimentation in addition to the wounds of the economic crisis itself. The reforming Emperors of the late third and early fourth centuries decided that the only way of economic salvation was to insist on an unalterable system of social functionalization. This meant that everyone stayed in the position in the social and economic hierarchy in which he had been born. The middle classes in particular, the so-called *curiales*, were charged with the task of perpetual tax-collecting and were themselves held responsible for the presentation of the total sum. If they were unable to collect all that was assessed by the authorities, they were held personally responsible for the outstanding balance. All attempts to escape this dubious honour were frustrated and the ruin of the middle classes was completed. By the fourth century the miserable *curiales* were fleeing wholesale from the still further shrinking towns and trying to achieve a welcome anonymity in the countryside or perhaps even deserting to the barbarians. In the fifth century, Salvian, a Christian polemicist writing with the purpose of describing the sorry state to which Rome's vices have brought it, singles out the oppressive weight of taxation as one of the main reasons for the decay of Roman society. The existence of the fifth-century towns was crawling on slowly and sordidly, still victim of the policy inaugurated by Diocletian; among their citizens, too, as many as could return to the land did so.

It is evident, then, that a profound *bouleversement* in favour of a society more preponderantly agrarian than ever was taking place, and that this *bouleversement* was primarily due to an upsurge of protracted pressure from internal and external peasant forces, operating through control of the military machine. It has recently been argued by Professor A. H. M. Jones that the collapse of the Empire was primarily due to increased external pressure on an extensive frontier line. We might be tempted to take the argument a stage further and suggest that the key factor in the Imperial collapse was the passing of control of the Empire's military arms to men for whom the old social traditions of Rome meant little. The fall of the Western Empire may have been, as Gibbon maintained, due to the 'triumph of barbarism and Christianity', but it also owed something to the actions of a long submerged peasantry.

The peasantry of the third to fifth centuries were uncertain about aims and desperately short of constructive leadership; they produced no Lenin. The importance of the 'Green Revolution' which they heralded cannot, however, be overestimated, though few accounts of the Middle Ages show a due appreciation of it. It is no exaggeration to say that the steady advance of the peasantry to greater control of the land forms one of the main motifs of European history down to the Industrial Revolution – and even beyond, in countries where the Industrial Revolution had less effect. In this long story the Middle Ages plays an essential part. We shall see in more detail later how the peasantry succeeded against all probable odds in obtaining a share, albeit precarious, in legal ownership of the land side by side with the aristocracy itself – a development unparalleled in any other civilization.

The peasant question mark and the peasant voice, muted though it inevitably had to be for the most part, was a major and menacing medieval theme. One is reminded of Hegel's 'lordship and bondage' theory where it is argued that a mutually necessary relation develops between legal master and legal dependant, the real dependency being not only on the one side; for the master needs the dependant just as much as the latter needs the master. This situation certainly applied in the Middle Ages, and had already been realized by St Augustine in discussing the master-servant relationship:

He [the servant] needs the good you provide for him in feeding him, and you need the good he provides for you by his service. For yourself you cannot do all the drawing of water, the cooking, the running before your carriage, the grooming of your beast. You are in want of the good your servant furnishes, you are in want of attendance; and inasmuch as you want an inferior, you are no true lord.[1]

The development of the agrarian structure, which made slave labour uneconomic, created a large group of peasant tenants without whose labour the great estates of feudal type could not have existed.

The relationship thus created remained ambivalent throughout the period. On the one hand nobles and clerics vied with each other in despising the peasantry as uncultivated, unheroic beings, engrossed in their material background to the point of sin; the terrified repulsion inspired by the peasant is illustrated by an extract from *Aucassin and Nicolette*, the early thirteenth-century Provençal romance. The young aristocratic Aucassin, in search of his lost love Nicolette, meets a rather caricatured but still remarkably lifelike peasant in the course of his wanderings through the forest. This is how the Provençal writer described the peasant for his aristocratic audience:

Tall he was, and marvellously ugly and hideous. His head was big and blacker than smoked meat; the palm of your hand could easily have gone between his two eyes; he had very large cheeks and a monstrous flat nose with great nostrils; lips redder than uncooked flesh; teeth yellow and foul; he was shod with shoes and gaiters of bull's hide, bound about the leg with ropes to well above the knee; upon his back was a rough cloth; and he stood leaning on a huge club. Aucassin urged his steed towards him, but was all afeared when he saw him as he was.[2]

1. *In Epistola Ioannis*, viii, 14. Translation by J. Burnaby, *Amor Dei*, p. 327.
2. Translation by Eugene Mason, *Aucassin and Nicolette and Other Medieval Romances and Legends*, Everyman Library edition, p. 24.

The conversation of the noble and peasant is illuminating and reveals that the Provençal author was not altogether unsympathetic towards the peasant's case. To Aucassin, who conceals the true object of his quest by making out that he is looking for a lost hound, the peasant replies by a moving list of grievances:

I was hired by a rich farmer to drive his plough, with a yoke of four oxen. Now three days ago, by great mischance, I lost the best of my bullocks, Roget, the very best ox in the plough. I have been looking for him ever since, and have neither eaten nor drunk for three days, since I dare not go back to the town, because men would put me into prison, as I have no money to pay for my loss. Of all the riches of the world I have nought but the rags upon my back. My poor old mother, too, who had nothing but one worn-out mattress, why, they have taken that from under her, and left her lying on the naked straw. That hurts me more than my own trouble. . . .[3]

The story is sufficient to move Aucassin to the point of giving the peasant money to compensate for his loss. This movement of responsibility of rich for poor, noble for peasant is paralleled in more theoretical form by John of Salisbury in his *Policraticus* (c. 1160) in his famous analogy of the body politic to the human body. John compares peasants to

the feet which always cleave to the soil, and need the more specially the care and foresight of the head, since while they walk upon the earth doing service with their bodies, they meet the more often with stones of stumbling, and therefore deserve aid and protection all the more justly since it is they who raise, sustain, and move forward the weight of the entire body.[4]

Much later, almost contemporaneously with the English Peasants' Revolt of 1381, William Langland's *Piers Plow-*

3. ibid., p. 25.
4. Translation by J. Dickinson.

man, again coming from a sympathetic clerical source, reiterates the same theme of the necessity of compassion –

> The needy are our neighbours, if we note rightly:
> As prisoners in cells, or poor folk in hovels,
> Charged with children and overcharged by landlords . . .
> It were an alms to help all with such burdens,
> And to comfort such cottages and crooked men and blind folk.[5]

The attitude of these literary clerics was that of a minority. The more typical outlook would be that of the denunciation of peasants as a congenitally evil class by many medieval preachers and the rank contempt felt by many nobles for the clodhoppers on whom they depended so much. Andreas Capellanus, author of a manual of courtly love, tells his readers that if they desire physical possession of a peasant girl, they need not waste time in elaborate approaches; it is quite in order to take the girl by force.

Faced by this oppression, the peasants' reply was a sullen resentment punctuated by outbreaks of terrifying violence. The Revolt of 1381 with its slogan –

> When Adam delved and Eve span,
> Who was then the gentleman?

is a particularly famous example; the French Jacquerie a little earlier in the same century was longer and bloodier. At the end of the medieval period the Peasants' War in Germany in the 1520s provided the biggest holocaust of all and the same pattern can be followed down to the Russian and Chinese Revolutions of contemporary times. It has been pointed out that a feature of these violent outbursts of Europe's protracted 'Green Revolution' was a belief in an apocalyptic transformation of

5. Translation by H. W. Wells.

an existing corrupt society, usually by a Messianic figure who might be either a reincarnation of a famous past hero, such as Charlemagne or Frederick Barbarossa, or a figure of salvation known only to the future. Norman Cohn in his brilliant account of the medieval underworld of myth and fantasy, *The Pursuit of the Millenium*, has attempted with some degree of success to trace the ancestry of modern totalitarian theories of dictatorial leadership to this period of medieval social turmoil, while the continuity of the connexion between apocalyptic fantasy and the resentment of a submerged social class has been shown in the modern case histories collected by Vittorio Lanternari in his *Religions of the Oppressed*. But, when all has been said, the lot of the medieval peasant usually demanded not desperate heroism but the perhaps more exacting brand of everyday endurance. Nature and Man alike often seemed to have conspired against him, but, despite the monotony of the one and the legalistic cruelty of the other, the peasant slowly increased his control over his land.

The barbarian beneficiaries of the dying Western Empire took several centuries before achieving a permanent distribution of the spoils. The infiltration of the third and fourth centuries began to enter a more overt and dangerous phase with the arrival of whole nations, complete with arms and womenfolk. The battle of Adrianople in 378, when the Visigoths destroyed a Roman army and killed its Emperor, awoke the Roman world to its danger, but there was no time for redeployment. From 406 onwards, when on a winter night the Sueves and Vandals poured across the frozen Rhine into Gaul, the Western Empire's fate was within sight. In 410 the Visigoths sacked Rome itself; the comparatively gentle rape of the mistress of the world acquired a symbolism perhaps out of proportion to its practical significance. The fact that Rome could fall at all seemed to the Latin world to be an indication that the end of civilization, if not of the world itself, was at hand.

But Latin culture had more life in it than its members suspected. The incoming barbarians hesitated in the midst of their destructive orgy; the spell of the old Empire, impressive even as it was going to seed, was still powerful. Some Germanic tribes, like the Visigoths themselves, were already Christian, even if of an heretical persuasion, and they were beginning to see that there was more advantage to be gained in using rather than annihilating at any rate the outward trappings of Imperial government and administration. If Rome had not existed, it would have been necessary to invent her. The story of Atawulf, a king of the Visigoths, is typical. After toying for a time with the idea of abolishing the prostrate Empire and founding a Gothic Empire instead, he changed his mind, forced the Empire to legalize his own acquisition of the territory he had seized and capped all by marrying a Roman princess of the Imperial house.

The Atawulf pattern was followed by most of the other barbarian tribes. All over the Western world Roman law and Roman coinage, both in a debased form, continued to enjoy a respected position. After the extinction of the Western Empire in 476, the sovereigns of the 'other Rome' at Constantinople continued to be regarded as exercising some kind of loose suzerainty over the barbarian successor States, though the one attempt (that made by Justinian in the sixth century) to translate this suzerainty into governmental reality was bitterly opposed and finally failed after a mammoth expenditure of men and money.

By now the map of Europe was beginning to show

some resemblance to what was to be its medieval configuration. Italy, after Justinian had cleared it of the Ostrogoths, was invaded by another group of blond beasts, the Lombards, who secured control of most of the north and centre of the peninsula, leaving the Byzantines to maintain a bastion in the southern half of the country and the Pope in Rome to hover uneasily between the two. Gaul and a large chunk of Western and Southern Germany formed the biggest barbarian kingdom, that of the Franks, whose Merovingian kings had gone one better than the rest of their barbarian competitors by becoming orthodox Catholics. First ruffians and then puppets, the outstanding permanent contribution of the Merovingian dynasty was to lay the foundations of a Papal–Frankish axis which was to change the face of Western Europe.

North of the Channel the province of Britain had fallen into complete obscurity. Unlike the Continental barbarians, the Anglo-Saxon invaders of the island arrived as complete pagans and this tended to break the thread of continuity with Latin culture. The fifth and sixth centuries mark a progressive falling of the curtain of historical darkness over the once flourishing Roman–Celtic province. If ever King Arthur existed, it is to this dark period that he really belongs; but if he did, he was far different from the figure of romance who was to make his way from Geoffrey of Monmouth to T. H. White via Malory, Tennyson and Mark Twain. For the sixth-century Continental scholar and man of culture, the island of Britain was no gateway to Avalon; it was rather, as the Byzantine Procopius seriously avers, the gateway to Hell, the sinister abode to which the souls of the dead were ferried at night over from Gaul. Certainly the sixth century had no incentive to make the Channel crossing; but when Augustine finally did so in

597 he found the situation crystallizing not exactly into Hell but into England.

Spain had become the final home of the Visigoths. During the sixth century these too became Catholics and established a creditable sub-Roman culture within their sheltered peninsula. Their immunity met with a spectacular end in 711 and subsequent years with the Moslem invasion and conquest of Spain, which left the Visigothic Christian ancestors of modern Spain with a tiny foothold on the northern coast.

In the same year as the Moslems landed in Spain, they were battering, though with less success, at the gates of Constantinople. These two events marked geographically the two extreme horns of what may be described, if an easy pun may be overlooked, as a great crescent of Moslem expansion round the southern half of the Mediterranean from Asia Minor to the Atlantic. The explanation of the great Arabic conquests is still debated among historians. The social pressure of hunger always endemic in the Arabian peninsula seems to have linked up in the immediate pre-Islamic period with a more efficient tribal organization, which in turn produced a more effective military machine; but it was the appearance of a dynamic new religious ideology centred on the personality of Mohammed himself which provided the crucible to fuse all these elements. This was not the last time that a combination of such factors was to sweep the political board in the Arabian peninsula; in our own century the meteoric rise to ascendancy of Ibn Saud and his dynasty is an example of the strange continuities of history which, after all, may sometimes repeat itself.

What consequences for Western Europe flowed from the Islamic conquest of the Southern Mediterranean? All the discussion on this subject is now conditioned by

the work of Henri Pirenne, the famous Belgian historian, who argued in a succession of books and articles,
and particularly in his *Mohammed and Charlemagne*,
that the Islamic conquests, by closing the Mediterranean to the Christian West as a trading area and forcing
Latin Christendom to be a land-locked agricultural
economy, dealt the final blow to the ancient Roman
world and provided the true starting-point for the Middle Ages. The essential continuity of the barbarian
world with that of Rome had already been argued by a
number of scholars, particularly the Austrian Alfons
Dopsch, but Pirenne now claimed that it was the Islamic impact which really put an end to the unified
Mediterranean culture of the Roman Empire. Pirenne
laid great stress on the continuation of the trading tradition of the Roman money economy period in Merovingian Gaul and alleged that this was largely replaced
by a barter economy and virtual cessation of trade in
the West after the Islamic conquests. Pirenne's theory
has been strongly criticized. It has been questioned
whether the Merovingian economy was so essentially
continuous with Rome in its financial and trading
structure as he claimed; there is in fact a good deal of
evidence which suggests that there was an economic recession during the Merovingian period due to the governmental incompetence of the Frankish kings in this
as in other fields. The abandonment of the right of minting coinage into private hands, which is what the Merovingians actually allowed, is hardly evidence of a sound
economy; nor would the presence of Syrian merchants
in the West be conclusive evidence of a wholesale continuation of trading life. The partial collapse of urban
vitality to which we have previously referred would indeed point in the opposite direction. One of Pirenne's
most formidable critics, Robert Latouche, has in fact

argued in his brilliant book, *The Birth of Western Economy*, that the Carolingians, far from retreating to a land-locked economy, promoted economic recovery by their monetary reform and their control of economic development in countryside and town.

Perhaps the economic impact of Islam on the West was not as radical as Pirenne believed; but yet the Islamic presence was to be a constant feature of the medieval landscape. This was true of many levels of medieval Western man's consciousness. On the basic and fundamental level, Islam remained the arch-enemy of the Faith to which Western Europe had now given its allegiance. Over the centuries the physical fight against the heathen assumed the character of the fundamental enterprise of secular Christian society, a simple interpretation of Christian duty which was only too congenial to the fighting spirit of barbarian and feudal society. The outlook of the warrior nobility of the Dark Ages was foreshadowed in Clovis's famous outburst when hearing of the Crucifixion of Christ at his conversion in 496: 'This would not have happened if I had been there with my Franks!' This missing of the point of the Redemption doctrine was repeated by numerous Christian crowned heads of the period. The forcible baptism of defeated pagans by Charlemagne, Olaf Tryggvason of Norway and even the enlightened Alfred the Great is indicative of the trend towards force in the propagation of Christian belief, a trend which had seemed so alien to the early Church. And though the new strong-armed attitude was applied to all non-Christians, it was to Islam that it was applied above all. *The Song of Roland* (twelfth century) states boldly –

> Christians are right,
> Pagans are wrong

but the pagans it has in mind are the ever-present menacing hordes of Islam, and the symbol of the Christian warrior which medieval Christian noble society revered was Roland himself, holding the Pass of Roncesvalles almost single-handed against the overwhelming numbers of Moslem opponents.

The famous epic, besides being a perfect expression of the feudal military *ethos* (of which more in another chapter) was of course a product of the heart of the crusading era. The crusading concept itself owed something to Islam's own conception of a *jihad*, or 'holy war', though the Christian warriors at first carried the principle a stage further. Whereas Islamic conquerors had been content to exact financial tribute from their subject populations of alien religion, the frightful massacres attending the First Crusade bore witness to a more ruthless policy of extermination by the Westerners. After the settlement of the Europeans in the artificial and strategically unviable Kingdom of Jerusalem in the twelfth century, a more relaxed policy gained ground and the Christian rulers of the Near East, while they survived, became more and more assimilated to their Moslem background. The same process is observable in other borderlands of mixed Christian and Islamic culture, notably Spain (where we have an arresting account from the eleventh century of a Christian noble in Catalonia reclining in the midst of his harem complete with Moorish costume) and Southern Italy, where the Norman and Hohenstaufen dynasties in turn indulged in a progressive Arabization of manners and customs.

This 'velvet glove' attitude towards Islam was also reflected among theologians. Even in the twelfth century, at the height of crusading zeal and success, Peter the Venerable, Abbot of Cluny, was urging study of

Islamic religion, language and politics as a prelude to an alternative programme of peaceful conversion rather than forcible extermination. The perversion of the crusading ideal into aberrations such as the attack on the Byzantine Empire in 1204 led to the weakening of the faith in it as an instrument of Christian policy, while the progressive reconquest by Islam of the Christian Near Eastern territories showed that even as a military weapon the Crusade was a spent force. Yet it was hard to abandon it completely as a communal emotive force, and the resurgence of Islamic strength in the late medieval period, particularly with the appearance of the Ottoman Turks in the Near East and the Balkans, tended on numerous occasions, though usually with ultimate fiasco, to ring the alarm bells of renewed attempts at revived crusading activity.

At the same time the West was prepared to learn from Islam. Both in matter and technique of intellectual activity there was much in common between medieval Latin Christianity and medieval Islam, perhaps paradoxically more than between Latin and Greek Christianity. Both religions were concerned with the problem of the correct relationship between revelation and reason, and both were concerned with the implementation of religious faith as the dynamic of social order. Under these circumstances a strange love-hate relationship towards Islam can be traced in the Western medieval outlook. Dante certainly voiced a common opinion when he consigned Mohammed to Hell as one of the chief of the religious deceivers and the personality of the Prophet had to wait until the seventeenth century to get any favourable appreciation in the West. On the other hand, the virtues of Islam, particularly its monotheism, were frequently acknowledged and some Christian thinkers, like Nicholas of Cusa in the fifteenth century, were hopeful that this factor could form a starting-point for a dialogue between the faiths which could advance from disagreement to union. Nearly two centuries before Nicholas, the enigmatic Catalan mystic Ramon Lull had worked out what he regarded as an infallible system of logical proof which would not fail to convince intellectually open-minded Moslems, while, for the less mentally agile rank and file of Islam, the French lawyer Pierre Dubois (early fourteenth century) suggested that the importation into Islamic lands of a sufficient number of attractive Christian women would pave the way for conversion. Whatever their feuds, military or intellectual, the sense of family relationship between Christianity and Islam remained a powerful, if ambiguous factor in the moulding of the Western European attitude to the non-European world. The medieval rivalry of Bible and Koran cannot be forgotten in assessing the origins of modern European attitudes to other creeds and colours.

The final wave of barbarian settlement broke over Europe in the ninth and tenth centuries, just as it seemed that Charlemagne and his successors had solved the problem of European political disunity by imposing the rule of their own dynasty. In the East the Magyars, a nomadic warrior race of Central Asian extraction, galloped into the plains between the Carpathians and the Danube and became the permanent occupants of that area. After several decades of raids into Christian Germany they were finally contained in what is now Hungary by Otto the Great (955) and became within a comparatively short period a settled agricultural and Christian people, involved in a direct relationship with the Papacy through the conferring of the title of King on St Stephen, the Hungarian Constantine. The transformation served to emphasize the success of Latin Christianity in its programme of conversion of the barbarian successor States to the Roman Empire.

The Vikings from Scandinavia were a tougher proposition. As seafarers they were able to preserve a separate cultural identity to a more considerable extent than the Magyars, and for the same reason their inroads were more widespread and more destructive. At the same time, once they had been brought within the orbit of the Christian European community, they brought to it their own characteristic contribution. They were not merely destructive pirates. As daring explorers they sailed the Atlantic, colonized Iceland and almost certainly reached the North American Continent; as rulers and administrators they created new States in Russia, Normandy, England and Southern Italy; their keen sense of synthesis between governmental responsibility and individual initiative led in the two last mentioned lands to the creation of centralized systems of administration unparalleled elsewhere in medieval Europe. Finally, as traders and merchants they opened up new lines of economic development in both Eastern and Western Europe. It has been suggested that their activities in this sphere were a contributory factor to the economic revival of the tenth and following centuries.

The racial and geographical constituents of medieval Europe were complete by the eleventh century. We must now investigate the deeper social forces which created a homogeneous community out of this welter of diverse elements.

THE DILEMMAS OF MEDIEVAL
CHRISTIANITY

THE bald decline of the expected moment of Christ's
Second Coming faced the early Church from the second
century on with an unavoidable reappraisal of its position both with regard to its relation with the outside
world and also in its own interior discipline. The kernel
of Christian faith and life was the intensely personal relationship of the saved believer with his Saviour, but
the New Testament itself indicates that from the start
the believers also felt a sense of corporate identity and
that this community of redeemed souls needed as its
outward medium of expression some institutional
framework. The leadership of local bishops, which
Christians of the early ages linked with the tradition of
sacramental descent from the Apostles by ordination
and consecration, was the pattern of Christian internal
government, and significantly enough the headquarters
of the bishop usually corresponded to the political seat
of government of his area. The name 'diocese', which
was to become the specific term designating a bishop's
area of authority, was borrowed from Roman Imperial
nomenclature.

By the time of Constantine's conversion the Church
had assumed the form of a highly articulated governmental institution. Its capacity for institutionalization
was to stand it in good stead in the Middle Ages. It enabled it to rise above the chaos of the barbarian invasions and later to incarnate the juridical values of
Rome more than any other medieval institution. In ad-

dition, the watchdog function of the hierarchy and more particularly the Papacy managed to prevent the Christian community of the West from being splintered into various sects giving partial if not distorted presentations of the Christian Gospel. The problem of heresy was far from absent in early Christian days; the wild aberrations of fantasy of the Gnostic schools of the second and third centuries, with their allegorizing of the historical Christ and His message into mythological systems of philosophical symbolism, would have changed if not abolished traditional Christianity had there been no official organ of the Church to proclaim what was true and false doctrine. The Albigensian heresy of the thirteenth century, with its pessimistic dualism and its hatred of the body and of matter, was another doctrinal antithesis to orthodox Christianity and it is difficult to see what the latter could do but condemn it. This much seems clear, whatever one's opinion about the often brutal and repulsive methods used by the medieval Church to implement its condemnation.

The attitude of orthodox Christianity towards the practical combating of heresy changed in much the same way as its attitude to war. Early Christians down to the fourth century had deprecated any form of bodily coercion of heretics; it was the Christianized Emperors themselves, such as Theodosius I, who were to lead the way to an intolerant outlook. St Augustine was prepared to allow a measure of physical pressure for the good of the orthodox Church and State, but still shrank from the death penalty. During the period up to the twelfth century it was usually popular outbursts rather than official policy which led to massacres or atrocities against heretics or infidels. Only in the thirteenth century did a programme of persecution receive full official blessing with the creation of the Inquisition as a discip-

linary and repressive tribunal, while St Thomas Aquinas,
liberal-minded in many ways as he was, was prepared to
argue in favour of the death penalty for heretics, regard-
ing their desertion of the Church as a parallel to treason
against the civil community. Even at this stage, however, Aquinas still maintains a distinction between
heretic and infidel; the former may justifiably be penal-
ized for having forsaken their baptismal promises
(though Aquinas ignores the fact that these promises
had in any case usually been made by proxy in the in-
fancy of the baptized person). Infidels, on the other
hand, had never been part of the Church's community,
so there were no grounds for using aggressive force
against them. In practice the Jews in Western Europe
in the medieval period often had cause to be grateful
to the Papacy and the bishops for protecting them from
mob fury.

Widespread and deep as was the articulation of Christianity in an organized institutional framework, the element of emphasis on individual personality was equally
great. This element, we may safely guess, was the real
cause of Christianity's final ascendancy in the Roman
world. It is true that other historically measurable
causes were also at work. Historians of the fourth century seem to have established that there was a tendency
for Christian converts in the West to come from the
middle classes and the Imperial bureaucracy, while the
aristocracy clung very much longer to pagan tradition
and the peasants were even later in catching up with the
spiritual revolution which was taking place (though in
North Africa the Donatist form of Christianity seems to
have served as a vehicle of social revolt). It also seems
that Christianity at this period was at its most thriving
in the cosmopolitan atmosphere of the towns. But some-

thing deeper than these social or geographical factors is necessary to explain what happened.

The fundamental explanation of the rise of Christianity, it may be suggested, was the ancient world's craving for a more deeply personal relationship of the individual to his natural and supernatural environment than could be provided by the city State or the Imperial framework. As Weber pointed out in his book, *The City* (the arguments of which have stood the test of time better than his more famous thesis on Protestantism and the rise of Capitalism), the ancient city was a combination of groups (tribes, families, trades) rather than of individuals, and it seems likely that the reaction in the period between Alexander and Constantine towards more 'personalist' philosophies (Stoicism, Epicureanism, Neo-Platonism) was a measure of the frustration of the individual with the collectivist framework of his social life. Even the 'Mystery Religions' which approached Christianity most nearly in providing faiths of individual salvation for the regenerate believer, did so through the medium of restricted social groups; thus Mithraism was a religion for soldiers and admitted no women. Christianity alone, with its gospel of the salvation or damnation of the individual according to his acceptance or rejection of a unique personal relationship with God, appealed to the individual regardless of class, group, nation or sex; by hiving off from its parent Judaism it had freed the religion of the Old Testament from the ethnic exclusiveness which was the chief barrier to its propagation among the Gentiles. The Christian believed that he stood in an intimate relationship to a definite historical Person, who though divine, was yet indisputably flesh and blood; the triumphant cry of St Paul, 'But now I live, yet not I, but Christ liveth in me,' expressed a mood of personal union felt by every sincere believer and beside which abstract loyalty to city or Empire seemed a pale abstraction. In many other directions, as we shall see in a subsequent chapter, the society of the later Empire was moving in the direction of emphasis on personal relations as the basis for all social institutions. Christianity was at once expression and cause of this movement, which we may confidently single out as the fundamental distinguishing mark of Western culture. We need not be as surprised as Gibbon was to find barbers and mechanics of the fourth century becoming passionately involved in the Trinitarian controversy, for that controversy itself was a theological elucidation of the nature of personality and personal relations within the Godhead itself, a bold exploration which finds no parallel in any other religion before or since. The Christological controversies of the fifth century stem from the same impetus – this time the need for clarification of the Personality of the Divine Redeemer, God the Son.

Early Christian art shows the same preoccupation in more tangible form. The traditional classic 'Attic' type of artistic representation, with its emphasis on the impersonal and idealized qualities of an abstract human perfection, made little appeal to Christian artists in the West (though it did inspire much of Byzantine art). The belief of the Church in original sin and human fallibility (emphasized more in the West than the East) made it look elsewhere for art forms which would combine a realistic appraisal of corrupted human nature with the spiritual hope of human redemption through Christ. The so-called 'Alexandrian' school, more addicted to picturesque and romantic detail, helped Christian artists to give more play to their interest in concentration on the individual person with his unique peculiarities,

but the 'expressionist' school, originating in the East
but dominant in Rome by the fourth century, provides the best example of the individualist twist
given by Christianity to art. As a specimen we may mention the striking example (from the Catacombs in Rome)
where we can see the mother and child depicted (they
may even be Christ and His Mother themselves) staring
out of the picture as if looking into some reality beyond the external spatial framework in which they are
placed. The faces and their expressions may be said
to symbolize the dilemma of Christianity as soon as it
had become clear that the eschatological *dénouement*
which early Christianity had regarded as imminent was,
on the contrary, receding into an indefinite future. The
longer the Second Coming was delayed, the more it became inescapable for Christianity to reach a *modus
vivendi* with a stubbornly continuing, if corrupt, world.
No one was more aware of the dilemma than St Augustine of Hippo (354–430) and no one fought so consist-
ently to find an answer to it. He, more than anyone
else, formulated the lines along which the Western
world was to move in reconciling the Christian, Roman
and Germanic elements which were to be its principal
constituents.

Before Augustine such a reconciliation might well have
seemed to be impossible. Christianity had been accused
by paganism as being, by its alleged fanatical exclusiveness, incompatible with the reasonable balance of
the Graeco-Roman classical ideal. Only a small group
of Christian apologists, the Alexandrian group of Clement and Origen, had attempted seriously to controvert
this. The more usual attitude of educated Christians had
been a mixture of attraction and repulsion towards the
old cultural tradition. St Jerome's nightmare, when he

was indicted by his supernatural visitor as being a Ciceronian rather than a Christian, is typical of the dilemma; the classical writings, with their false religious views and their downright lasciviousness, were felt to be alluringly dangerous precisely because they made such good reading. Yet they could not be dispensed with, for they were the only feasible means of education, even for a Christian society such as the Roman world was rapidly becoming. There may have been some Christians who shared in advance the exasperated extremism of St Gregory the Great, who was to brand a Gaulish bishop as being wellnigh an unbeliever because he had taken pains to obey the rules of Latin grammar. But the ultimate majority of educated Christians preferred a compromise solution which would leave a suitably censored classical literature at the disposal of the new society.

Augustine was largely responsible for the success of this moderate solution. In his *De Doctrina Christiana* he takes as an analogy the spoiling of the Egyptians by the departing Israelites as recounted in Exodus. Augustine interprets this as a licence to Christianity to extract for its own use whatever may be of service from classical culture. Thus he has no hesitation in recommending Christians to avail themselves if necessary of the rhetorical studies which still formed the staple of Roman education. Admittedly he preferred to make use of the literary material provided by the Scriptures wherever practicable, but his suggestions could in principle be applied to pagan writers also and in fact were so applied by later medieval scholars. It is true to say that Augustine's readiness to pillage classical culture was accentuated by a temperamental inability to achieve a clear distinction between reason and revelation. Convinced of the impossibility of man's achieving anything good by himself, Augustine seems to have believed that the simplest processes of ratiocination had to depend at every stage on the sustaining direct illumination of God. In this background the minutest earthly happening assumed a direct relationship to the Divine government of the universe, and in conformity with a general tendency in his age common to Christian and pagan alike Augustine looked at the material world in symbolical rather than causal or analytical terms. Every object, animate and inanimate, has its symbolical meaning in the cipher book of the universe, and the real function of Christian education is to provide training in the appreciation of this universal riddle. Both scriptural and profane literature are to be interpreted according to this standard of allegorical interpretation. Augustine does not, it is true, pursue his own tenets into the realm of often ludicrous, if logical, fantasy to the same extent as did some of his disciples. There is nothing in Augustine to parallel Gregory the Great's comparison of the Emperor to the ugly, if virile, rhinoceros, or that of later phallically minded medieval symbolists who transformed the actually existing one-horned tropical beast into the half-mystical, half-erotic unicorn who could only be tamed when he found his resting-place in the lap of a pure virgin. Nevertheless, his emphasis on the place of allegory in human knowledge led to profound influences on the medieval approach to all the arts and sciences. A search for pattern and correspondence took possession of the aesthetic sense of Christendom. This by no means rules out realistic observation. The Gothic cathedral, as it now seems clear, owed much of its design to the geometrical symbolism which Augustine had derived from the Platonic tradition and which he passed on to the Middle Ages by way of his *De Musica*. Yet by comparison with the realism of the decorations, sculptured or painted, produced by medieval Gothic, later and more self-conscious 'imitation of nature' might be thought painfully laboured. The truth seems to be that the symbolical pattern which the medieval outlook imposed on the universe may have heightened rather than diminished the importance of the individual in art; even the ugliest and lowest of creatures could now assume, thanks to the symbolic value incarnated in him, a dignity which he had not hitherto possessed. In the realm of art, as in other spheres, the recognition of personality forms the hallmark of the medieval genius.

So Christianity was making its choice of collaboration, although on its own terms, with classical culture. But a further problem remained. With the barbarians swarming over the West, as they did in Augustine's lifetime, was it possible that any culture at all would survive? Hitherto both Christian and pagan Westerners had tended to equate the survival of Rome with the survival of civilization. A third-century Christian writer like Commodian might see the Goths as bringing the just punishment of God upon the wicked civilization which had rejected Christianity; but the almost universal Christian identification of the Empire with the enigmatic restraining force against Antichrist mentioned in St Paul's Second Epistle to the Thessalonians led less wholeheartedly apocalyptic Christians to look with some trepidation to the prospect of Rome's fall. St Jerome cannot have been alone in his lamentation after the sack of Rome in 410: 'The most brilliant light of the whole earth has been extinguished and the head of the Roman Empire has been severed ... the whole world has perished with this single city.' Augustine could not rest content with this view. Even before beginning to write the *City of God* (between 413 and 426) he was feeling his way towards a conception of Rome as being only an incident, albeit an important one, in the Providential march of universal history. And because Providence was primarily concerned with the salvation of individuals, history itself must be primarily a record of the encounters of individuals with God.

From this standpoint of individualism Augustine approaches the role of the State. For him society, even Roman society, is above all a collection of *temporarily* (the italics are very necessary) like-minded individuals: 'Perchance Rome will not perish if the Romans do not perish ... for what is Rome but the Romans?' The character of the State is determined by the character of its citizens.

This individualism seems to me to be the key to Augustine's whole scheme of thought, including his political philosophy. It may be objected that this is in conflict with the emphasis of Augustine's theology on collective guilt, transmitted by the heritage of Original Sin from generation to generation, since the fall of Adam. The conflict, is, however, more apparent than real, because Augustine's whole point is that the gift of individual responsibility, inherent in man because of his nature, was corrupted by the fall which made man dependent on malevolent influences which could come either from his own fellow men or from Nature or from superhuman demonic beings. It is only the grace of God, made available to the baptized Christian through Christ's redemption, which can restore the individual to the freedom which rightly belongs to him as originally created. The individual remains face to face with God in the centre of the stage. Perhaps enough has been said to indicate that here, too, the individual and his destiny form the pivot of Augustine's thinking.

Augustine's intensely individualist emphasis followed from the vividly personal struggle for spiritual certainty which is portrayed by him in the *Confessions*, a book unique in Graeco-Roman literature as an attempt at a spiritual and intellectual autobiography. From his family background divided between a pagan father and strictly Christian mother, Augustine inherited a tension which was confirmed by the turbulent development of his own early life. Augustine seems to have felt from the first the force of Christian claims but was prevented from accepting them for a long time for both intellectual and moral reasons. Even after reaching a point where he was convinced of the intellectual truth of Christianity, Augustine felt himself unable to become a Christian because of powerlessness to accept the religion's moral precepts ('O Lord, give me chastity, but not yet'), and it was only in 387 that he finally took the step of receiving baptism. The famous story of Augustine's conversion, as told in the *Confessions*, leaves no doubt that he regarded his conversion as due to direct Divine inspiration, without which his own will would have been unable to take the decisive step. This personal experience was believed by him to be but one example of an antithesis which ran right through human life since the Fall – the powerlessness and sin of Man contrasted with the grace and mercy of God. This antithesis was given institutional form, so to speak, in the *City of God*, in the symbolism of the Two Cities. The contrast and clash is best expressed in Augustine's own words in Book XIV: 'Two loves formed two cities; the earthly city was formed by love of self leading to contempt of God, the heavenly city was formed by .ove of God leading to contempt of self.'

The argument of the *City of God* has to be viewed in the context of the topical debate of the responsibility of Christianity for Rome's defeat by the Germanic barbarians. Augustine was not the only Christian writer to try to meet this challenge. But the apologists had tried to make out that the Roman world was, despite appearances to the contrary, more prosperous under Christianity than it had been before. Augustine himself abandoned this rather futile line and shifted the debate to a totally different plane, in which material prosperity and success were no longer the sole criterion.

History according to Augustine could only be understood and interpreted by reference to a standard outside itself – God's directing Providence. In Book V, Chapter II, Augustine argues that, if God controls Nature, it is unthinkable that 'the kingdoms of men, their governments and subjects are outside the laws of His Providence'. This theory of Providential government of history, which Christianity had inherited from Judaism, meant that the theory of cyclical process, which had dominated the thought of the classical world, had to be rejected. Mankind was no longer at the mercy of an endless alternation of different types of political régime, an alternation which the wise statesman could only retard, not change. Instead, history was now seen as a series of unique and unrepeatable events, each of which was part of a developing Divine plan towards a Divinely appointed destination. The first five books mark the fullest statement to date of a distinctively Christian philosophy of history. The significance of this change from viewing history as a circle to viewing it as a horizontal line is very important and to it may very well be traced all future theories of history seen in terms of unrepeatable development. Augustine stands at the head of a long line of European thinkers down to Marx and beyond.

Another aspect of this theory of history is what one might describe as a change in the conception of change itself. Classicism had tended to see change as something bad in itself, a sad consequence of the inexorable natural cycle. The Augustinian view of the Providential control of history meant that change need not be feared; on the contrary, being willed by God, it might even be beneficial.

From this overall viewpoint Augustine could afford to regard the fall of Rome with something approaching equanimity. To begin with, Rome was by him cut down to historical size. It was merely one, even if the greatest one, in a whole series of world empires raised up and thrown down by the Divine Will. Augustine was, however, prepared to give Rome her due, and Book V of the *City of God* contains what amounts to a balance-sheet of Rome's achievement. Augustine argues that Rome was built on the thirst for national glory inherent in the character of the early Romans: 'Glory was their supreme passion; for this they wished to live, for this they did not hesitate to die. All other desires they curbed in order to give rein to this absorbing ambition.' He explains this by saying that because their kingdom was earthly and not heavenly: 'What else could they have loved but glory? By means of glory they wished to enjoy even after death a kind of life in the praises of posterity.' And they did in fact

obtain their glory in almost all nations; upon many nations they imposed the laws of their empire, and today their glory is written in the literature and history of most nations. They have no reason to complain of the righteous justice of the all-high and true God; they have reaped their reward.

Augustine thus makes a clear-cut distinction between material and spiritual happiness, and political achievement thus collapses to a secondary plane. Great as Rome had been, its grandeur had been purely ephemeral; stability could not be found there, for true religion (that is, for Augustine, a correct view of the whole universal order seen from what approximated to the Divine perspective) was absent. Augustine, as we shall see, elaborates in Book XIX on this fatal flaw in pagan Roman society. But even in Book V we see him moving towards a conception of an ideal State in which political life will not be rejected but transfigured and purified by a Christian revolution. Augustine's description is in the tradition of a long line of classical writings on the ideal monarch, but with a Christianized flavour. The concrete cases which he chooses to cite as examples of his conception of a just monarch, Constantine and Theodosius, are not altogether happy when one considers them in a realistic historical context, but the main interest of Augustine's thought here is in his avoidance of any merely other-worldly doctrine of divorce from politics. Instead, he seems to be hinting that only Christianity can bring political development to its highest fulfilment. Here he points the way right into the heart of the Middle Ages.

In Book XIX of the *City of God* Augustine expresses in more detail than anywhere else his view on the relationship between the Christian and the secular community in which he finds himself.

This problem is for Augustine to be viewed in the light of his intensely individualist approach to human life – the relationship of the individual soul to God is for him the paramount consideration, and a right relationship to God is the only way of bringing stability and peace to the individual and therefore also to the community, which is made up of individuals. Augustine, as we have seen, holds no corporatist or organic view of the State as such. He speaks in Book XIX of 'social life' (*socialis vita*), but for him the phrase seems to be understood in its most literal sense, 'the life of friends', for in Chapter 5 and following he goes on to point out the essential imperfection of all human social connexions, from love to law. No human relationship, he argues, is free from discord or the fear of it. It goes without saying, he says confidently, that this applies to sexual love, whether in marriage or out of it, and often a person's worst enemies are the members of his own family. In the larger unit of the city civil strife is at any moment round the corner, while the law itself operates blindly and cruelly. 'One set of men passes judgement upon others whose consciences they are unable to see', – an almost anarchist protest by Augustine against the judgement of individual responsibility by the mechanical standards of a legal code. Looking outside the State one faces the melancholy spectacle of international disorder, only brought to an end by the dubious means of an imperialistically imposed peace under the autocratic rule of the strongest military power.

Yet, despite this apparent universal strife and frustration, Augustine contends paradoxically that the whole universe is directed, consciously or unconsciously, towards the achievement of peace. Even the disorderly and contending elements of the universe fight ultimately to obtain a peace which will satisfy their desires. Men fight wars not for their own sake but to obtain by suppressing their enemies an agreeable peace.

Those who are willing that the peace in which they live should be disturbed do not thereby show hatred of peace, but show their desire to alter it in accordance with their own wishes; they do not object to peace as such, but they want it to be such as they desire.[1]

1. Translation by R. A. Barrow, *An Introduction to St Augustine's City of God*, p. 86.

Thus even the desire for dominion over other men is a perverted expression of the desire for peace. Again one finds here a spirited protest by St Augustine in favour of the individual against arbitrary domination by other individuals. 'Pride,' he says,

distortedly imitates God. For it hates equality of fellow beings under Him; thus it hates the just peace of God and loves an inequitable peace of its own. It cannot do without loving peace of some kind. Indeed no corruption of good is so contrary to nature as to destroy even the last traces of nature.[2]

Peace, viewed in its positive sense, is for Augustine ordered contentment:

The peace of the body is ordered adjustment of its parts; the peace of the irrational parts of the soul is ordered rest from the appetites; the peace of the rational part of the soul is ordered correspondence of thought and action.

Augustine argues that Man, who alone possesses a rational soul, can therefore only obtain happiness if this rational soul acts as the principle of order and authority for the whole human being. The rational soul can only do this if it refers itself to the standard prescribed by Divine government and thereby reaches the stability impossible to achieve by purely earthly means.

Augustine is realistic enough, however, to insist that the quest for the stability which only the heavenly city can fully provide is to some extent limited by the conditions of earthly life. Temporal organization is necessary in the conditions of Christian pilgrimage through life on earth, even though by absolute standards (that is, what life would be if unaffected by sin and error) it is superfluous. The Christian loves God primarily, but this

2. ibid., p. 90.

does not blind him to his social responsibilities. Augustine sees the household or family as the most immediate of these responsibilities; he envisages a family group patriarchally governed by the husband in the traditional manner and regards this family unit as in some sense preparing its members for participation in the political life of the State. The household in fact takes its principles from the laws of the community in which it finds itself.

Augustine regards this paternally responsible government as the true type of political authority, and he is quite definite as to its 'conventional' or non-natural character. 'It was not His [God's] Will that Man, a creature possessed of reason and created in His image, should have dominion, unless over irrational creatures.'[3] This provides an approach to the problem of slavery which Augustine depicts as entirely due to sin, which itself introduced inequality among men. This being so, man had better make the best of a bad job. Augustine is no Abolitionist; he argues in Aristotelean or more likely Ciceronian terms that some men are better off as slaves; their servile status is more likely to preserve them from sin. Augustine argues that the head of the household may legitimately use force to correct his family or slaves when they do wrong.

Just as no one can claim to be a benefactor who by his active aid causes someone to lose a greater good, so no one can with a clear conscience spare a wrongdoer, and so allow him to fall into still greater evil.[4]

These words clearly lead the way into Augustine's view of the problem of State interference to enforce correct belief and hence to his observations on religious toleration. Augustine nowhere discusses this problem directly in

3. ibid., p. 100.   4. ibid., p. 104

the *City of God*, but we may find his opinion set forth in other writings of the same period.

His attitude towards the use of secular authority to enforce religious orthodoxy had progressively hardened since the early years of his conversion, when he had opposed any idea of coercion to spread true religion. By 409 he had altered his position perhaps under the stress of his years as a bishop in North Africa when one of his main preoccupations was opposition from the Donatist heretics, who were in fact first to appeal to physical force. We can trace the growing rigidity of his position in three letters. In the first, written in 409, Augustine merely asks for State action to prevent the Donatists from forcibly interfering with the Catholics, but enjoins the official to whom he writes to be lenient and not attempt forcible conversion : 'For the effort to make men abandon even a great evil and cleave to a great good produces more trouble than benefit, if they act merely under compulsion and not from conviction.'[5] By 411 Augustine is still urging moderation in the punishment of some Donatist militants who had been responsible for outrages against Catholics. In 416 Augustine has decided that force is legitimate to persuade a man to follow spiritual good. If a man may be forcibly prevented from committing temporal suicide, he argues, how much more may he be forcibly stopped from committing spiritual suicide? The words 'Compel them to come in' from the preamble to the parable of the wedding feast in St Luke's Gospel are twisted from their context by Augustine and taken to imply Divine support for a policy of persecution. It should be noted, however, that even in this final repressive period Augustine explicitly denounces the death penalty for heresy

5. Translation by J. Baxter, *The Letters of St Augustine*, Loeb Classical Texts, p. 189.

and still emphasizes his consistent point that punishment should be remedial and corrective. Granted this, it still remains true that in this matter Augustine exercised a fateful influence which later medieval society was not slow to follow.

Returning to Book XIX of the *City of God*, we find Augustine asserting that the heavenly city may make use of the peace provided by the earthly city. Augustine's view here would square with either a Christian or non-Christian State. In fact it would be an oversimplification of his picture of the two cities to suppose that the earthly city is to be equated in all circumstances with the State or, for that matter, the heavenly city with the Church. Augustine's thought is rather that the division between elect and damned, which is the fundamental distinction between the members of the two cities, overrides the visible earthly distinction between the Church and the State. Some members of the visible Church may in fact prove to be really members of the earthly city, while on the other hand the State, especially a Christian one, may include members of the heavenly city.

Nevertheless, in the final section of Book XIX, Augustine does elaborate a distinction between two types of State. The distinction takes the form of a discussion of Cicero's definition of a commonwealth in his *Republic*. Besides being an accepted classic of Roman political theory, the *Republic* seems to have had a particular vogue in Africa, to judge from the number of writers there who quote from it up to St Augustine's time.

Cicero had defined a commonwealth as a 'multitude of men united in fellowship by a common agreement as to what is just and by a common pursuit of interest'. Augustine argues that in point of fact Cicero's definition cannot be satisfied by any pagan State, because the essential attribute of justice is lacking to such a State precisely because it is pagan. Justice means rendering to everyone his due. But the pagan State subtracts from God the worship which is owed to Him, and so justice is lacking to it, and it cannot be called a commonwealth. Augustine substitutes as a definition of a State a formula of his own, running: 'A people is a gathering of a multitude of rational beings united in fellowship by sharing a common love of the same things.' 'To see the character of each people you have to examine what it loves.' This reformulation enables Augustine to bring the Roman and other pagan States within the scope of his definition, while eliminating justice from it.

This procedure has raised a lot of controversy among commentators. Does Augustine intend to divorce politics altogether from justice? Some commentators have found it incredible that Augustine should differ from every other writer of the classical world in being apparently prepared to contemplate political society without any reference to an absolute standard of right behaviour; a number of ingenious solutions have been suggested to avoid this apparent outcome. Others are prepared to take Augustine at face value, congratulating him on his realism in ruling out the element of value judgement from the analysis of the State. A third view holds that Augustine is not in fact speaking of any sort of earthly State when he talks of the true Christian commonwealth in which justice is present. He is thinking, on this interpretation, of the City of God itself, which for him is the only finally abiding entity. Politics in fact have become for him cosmology.

Whatever be the truth of what Augustine intended to mean here, there can be no doubt about what the Middle Ages made of it. For medieval Christian society the salient point of Augustine's doctrine in this section of the *City of God* was the linking of justice with Christianity and the consequent blurring of the distinction between sacred and secular. The Christian Commonwealth of the Middle Ages was neither exclusively a State nor a Church; it was both, an organism which included all members of the Western European community. Augustine's assertion of the necessity of a true commonwealth to be Christian was eventually interpreted to mean the dependence of all secular authority on the Church and finally on the Papacy. This so-called 'political Augustinism' had become the most dynamic element in European political thought by the thirteenth century. It is ironical that Augustine, with his emphasis on the significance of the individual and his depreciation of the importance of politics as a second-best result of sin, should have posthumously sponsored a theory which linked both politics and culture inseparably with a religious institutional system.

St Augustine's work had had the outcome of dissolving in the Christian mind the assumption that civilization could not survive without the continued existence of Rome. The spectre of Roman collapse had been canvassed in some Christian circles since the writing of the Apocalypse. In the third century the poet Commodian had first pointed to the German invaders as the destined agents of downfall, and the theologian Hippolytus had talked of new 'democracies' as superseding the Roman order. But it had been left for Augustine to spell out the concrete possibility of at least a *modus vivendi* between Christianity, civilization and the barbarian successor States to the Empire.

The new barbarian kingdoms for their part were touchingly anxious to vindicate for themselves a legitimate place in the conservation of order and civilization. The behaviour of the Visigothic invaders of Italy, France and Spain was a turning-point. After an initial hesitation the Visigothic kings decided to act as protectors rather than destroyers of the existing order; their consideration for the Latin majority of their subjects extended to accepting and adapting a version of Roman law (the so-called *Lex Romana Visigothorum*) for the use of their Roman citizens. The same procedure of separate legal treatment for Germans and Romans was followed with varying degrees of flexibility in the other Germanic Continental kingdoms.

The process of lasting political cohesion proved, however, to be ultimately beyond the powers of most of the new realms. Despite legal concessions the barriers between the politically dominant minority and the culturally superior majority were never fully broken down. And in all but one case a fundamental religious cleavage added its divisive effect to the picture of disunity. The Germanic tribes had been converted to Christianity before their conquest of the West. But the Christianity they had adopted had been the heretical Arian form and this left them permanently at loggerheads with their Catholic Latin subjects. There was no systematic persecution of the Catholics, except in Vandal Africa, but the underlying religious tension was bound to embitter racial relations, even when contained under the surface of the social fabric. An excellent illustration of the fundamental difficulties is provided by the experience of the Ostrogothic kingdom in Italy, founded by Theodoric the Ostrogoth in the confused struggles for power following the final official extinction of the Western Roman Empire in 476.

Theodoric's plan had originally been to preserve Gothic ascendancy by a system of alliances with other Germanic kingdoms but to conciliate the subject Roman

population by allowing them free exercise of their religion as well as their own legal system. He affected to
preserve Roman constitutional usage and to hold his
authority in Italy by virtue of delegation from the Emperor at Constantinople. Palaces and churches were constructed in the Romano-Byzantine style; Theodoric's
tomb at his capital, Ravenna, was built in imitation of
the mausoleum of the Emperor Hadrian (now the Castle
of St Angelo) at Rome. In many respects Theodoric's
realm seemed extremely well placed to become the first
successful instance of a genuinely coherent combination
of Roman and German elements. He needed his educated Roman subjects to enable the necessary wheels of
bureaucracy to continue to turn.

The career of Boethius, who became one of the most
significant names in medieval philosophy, is an example
of the tension which the new uncertain situation could
create in an educated and sensitive mind. Boethius, from
the upper-crust Senatorial Roman aristocracy, Catholic
and steeped in classical learning, seemed in every respect the epitome of the new educated Christian personality which Augustine had looked for. Besides assisting
in the political service of the new State, Boethius was
engaged on the ambitious intellectual enterprise of making available in Latin all the works of Plato and Aristotle. He came nowhere near completion of this task but
his translations of some of Aristotle's logical treatises
were to dominate the technique of intellectual argument
in the earlier medieval period and were to be foundation
stones of Scholasticism. In educational methodology
Boethius' handbooks on music, arithmetic and geometry were to form a similar milestone.
Beneath these successfully practical activities as
statesman and scholar, Boethius clearly felt the uncer-

tainties and ambiguities of his time and position. A poignant little poem indicates the tràgic dilemma in which he felt himself to be placed by conflicting claims upon his loyalties. In its *cri de cœur* we can catch a glimpse of the dilemma of the thoughtful Christian, caught in the maelstrom of the new society –

> What discord at the heart of things
> destroys the pact? What God has set
> this war between two truths, until
> singly they stand our test and yet
> together form a strife of will?
>
> Is truth a single harmony?
> Each life to its own purpose clings:
> and yet the flesh-entangled soul,
> using a smothered fire, can't see
> the subtle links that bind the whole.
>
> But why such anxious zeal to tear
> the mocking veils and look behind?
> Of what we seek, are we aware?
> Then why such toil if all is known?
> Yet otherwise the search is blind.
>
> What we've not known we cannot need,
> and unseen banner cannot lead.
> How could we find, or, having found,
> how shall we know we'd reached the goal?
>
> In contact with the great Alone,
> is it the whole or parts we mind?
> Though by our cloudy senses bound,
> the self has memories that endure.
> It drops the parts, yet grasps the whole.
>
> Then he who seeks the truth must fall
> on paradox. He'll neither grip
> nor yet forget, within, the All;
> but still he seeks the Truth he saw,

> to handle it and learn its law
> by adding truths that he let slip to those he
> kept secure.[6]

These lines may well have been occasioned by Boethius' sense of the tragic conflict inherent in the tension between the failing Roman tradition and its as yet uncouth successors, a tension which in the end would cost him his own life. But beneath this we may perhaps see the poem as an expression of an even deeper conflict within Boethius himself – a conflict between Christianity and a still unregenerate classical learning, a conflict which Boethius may have found to be more agonizing than either Jerome or Augustine had done. While Jerome exteriorized his conflicts in overtly expressed dreams and recantations, and Augustine found a way out by 'spoiling the Egyptians', Boethius could see no such clear-cut solution, and could only seek an uncertain relief by dividing his intellectual activity into two self-contained compartments. The same man who could write *De Fide Catholica* in orthodox exposition of the mysteries of the Christian Faith could also write *De Consolatione Philosophiae*, in which Christ and Christianity are not even mentioned.

Much of the atmosphere of the poem we have reproduced is Neo-Platonic rather than Christian. 'The Alone', the undifferentiated, unknowable, inaccessible Godhead had been familiar to the classical world since the days of Plato and Aristotle; in itself the conception was hardly reconcilable with the Christian discovery of God as a creative, loving Being. Boethius' use of the phrase is sufficient indication that he is literally a man of two traditions. Yet there is something here that is new to European poetry – the attempt to express in

6. Translation by Jack Lindsay, *Song of a Falling World*, pp. 241-2.

emotive language of great beauty the puzzling abysses of a divided human personality. Only Augustine had trodden this road before and he had only done so when he had already emerged from the abyss and could look back on it with a degree of security born from his readiness to throw in his lot decisively with one side of the intellectual arena. Boethius could not take this decisive action. For him the old traditions could not lightly be thrown over, and he had the nagging suspicion that perhaps they did not need to be either. Was Christianity as exclusive as some of its harder-minded adherents claimed? Boethius' dilemma was increased by the fact that by his time Rome and Catholicism were inextricably intertwined in the West, and it was becoming increasingly difficult to separate one from the other. Augustine might have proved that politically Rome was dispensable, but in the cultural field the opposite had been established in the century between him and Boethius.

It may well be significant that Boethius turns to the poetic medium to express the enigmas of personality as a mode of expression both vaguer and more flexible than the static definiteness of prose. Here again the contrast with Augustine, the prose writer *par excellence*, is instructive. Even in his *De Consolatione Philosophiae*, a largely prose work, Boethius cannot resist diverging into verse when he feels he must and in this he founded a lasting medieval tradition which was to extend down to the *fabliaux* and *Chansons* of Provence and France and the *Convivio* of Dante. Boethius is in fact the founder of the European tradition of introspective poetry. From now onwards poetic literature will be a vehicle, not only for the relation of great epic deeds or of the agonies and ecstasies of the love of man for woman, but for the exploration of individual doubts when face to face with the problem of universal meaning. Nor is it an accident that this poetry of tension, drama, debate should have its great periods of efflorescence at the most profound periods of intellectual and social disturbance in the history of the West. And this personal approach to reality, this obsessed and uniquely European fascination with the unsolved equation between personal perception and a baffling reality 'out there', this erection of doubt and uncertainty themselves into means for the attaining of an unexplored and probably surprising truth, find in Boethius their first and not least moving exponent. This sense of personality is the link between Boethius the logician and Boethius the poet. The definition of Person itself was formulated by Boethius and remained authoritative throughout the Middle Ages: 'The individual substance of a rational nature.'

The political dilemma in which he stood, the problem of Romano-Gothic coexistence, might be thought *sub specie aeternitatis* to have been the least fundamental of Boethius' problems. All the same, it proved to be the end of him. Imprisoned and under sentence of death by Theodoric for possible intrigue with Byzantium (scholars are appropriately enough divided in their opinion of whether or not Boethius really was guilty of the charge), Boethius wrote the *De Consolatione Philosophiae*, another of the basic classics of the Middle Ages. Translated into English by King Alfred and still more memorably by Chaucer, as well as into Old High German and French, the *Consolation of Philosophy* enumerates Boethius' doubts and ends by asserting belief in God's Wisdom as the ultimate resolver of all discrepancies.

Boethius' execution was the forceful expression of the breakdown of Theodoric's attempt at building a durable Romano-Germanic society. It was now only a matter of time before a revived Byzantium would reconquer Italy, albeit in Pyrrhic fashion, under Justinian, with the Latin Catholic population as an invariable Fifth Column. At the end of twenty years of bloody fighting the successors of Theodoric gave up the struggle and Theodoric himself faded into medieval legend as an exclusively Teutonic hero – Dietrich of Bern.

The other branch of the Gothic family, the Visigoths of Spain, was somewhat later in making its bid for the same social cohesion which had eluded the Ostrogoths. It was not until the end of the sixth century that the Visigothic kings perceived that acceptance of Catholicism was a *sine qua non* for obtaining the allegiance of the Hispano-Roman population. In fact, once the change to Catholicism had been made, the Visigoths seem to have led the way in bringing representatives of the clergy into direct participation in the ceremonial inauguration of a King. Apart from the obscure case of sixth-century Brittany, Visigothic Spain provides European history with the first example of a royal anointing ceremony.

In the following century the Spanish Visigothic realm showed promising signs of development. The first attempt at ending racial disunity by the acceptance of a legal code common to both German and Latin is to be found here, while Spain also provided, in the person of St Isidore of Seville, the first encyclopedist of medieval learning. It was technique which was the great merit of Isidore's arrangement; the clarity of his disposition of subject matter under appropriate headings appealed to the medieval mind as a convenient assistance in its search for knowledge. Though no Boethius, Isidore showed his feeling for the personal equation in the acquisition of learning by resting his whole methodology on the correct understanding of the meaning of words.

As we have seen, the Visigothic régime was brought to

a premature end by Moslem invasion and Spain was forcibly removed for several centuries from the mainstream of Western European development. It was left for a more northerly Germanic people to preside over the political and cultural integration which both branches of the Goths had vainly sought.

The Franks, a ruthless warrior people who first entered recorded history as dominators of a comparatively small area in what is now Flanders, would at first sight appear to have little qualification for success in such an exacting enterprise. By and large, a more individually unattractive succession of monarchs than the Merovingian royal dynasty would be hard to imagine. After the massive extension of their realm over the whole of the formerly Roman Gaul by Clovis, their founder and the one sovereign of ability to be produced by them, the history of the Merovingians is one of Wagnerian family feuding in the sixth century, to be followed by resigned acceptance of the role of crowned puppets in the seventh and eighth. The tiresome chronicle of their crimes and mistakes can be read in the pages of Gregory of Tours, and, even when allowance has been made for the exaggeration beloved of the medieval cleric when discussing the misdeeds of the laity, it is hard not to believe that Gregory needed to do no more than a little touching up.

The theory of Pirenne on the virtual continuance of Roman civilization by the Merovingian economic system has now met with grave challenge and few could accept the 'Pirenne thesis' in its complete form. Most scholars would now agree that Pirenne passed a far too indulgent judgement on the incompetent Merovingians and was correspondingly too harsh in his dismissal of the achievements of their Carolingian successors. The happiest stroke of the Merovingians was the decision of Clovis to accept Christianity in its Catholic form and thereby to remove at a blow the religious disharmony which bedevilled relations between rulers and ruled in the other Germanic kingdoms. It was only with the Carolingians, however, that the full political benefits of this conversion were reaped.

In the eighth century a momentous development occurred. After ruling the Frankish realm in fact though not in name, the Carolingian 'Mayors of the Palace', decided to turn their *de facto* dictatorship into *de jure* monarchical status. But they hesitated at outright setting aside of the rights of the Merovingian royal house. The latter had enjoyed a semi-divine magical status going back to the mists of the pagan ancestry of their race. The sea-god Meroveus had been their ancestor and this supernatural family tree gave an aura of sacrosanct authority to the dynasty which persisted in stubborn opposition to the contrast of the political impotence of its members in the seventh and eighth centuries. It has often been argued that this primitive 'Divine Right' of the Merovingians was just one example of a common Germanic view of kingship; but there is little evidence for this belief. The other leading Germanic monarchies changed their monarchs frequently enough and with little regard for hereditary status. The conclusion suggests itself that the Franks must have been distinguished from the start by an unusual emphasis on what we should call the 'legitimist' principle of monarchy, whatever the practical limitation on the monarchy's actual powers. This emphasis was in fact to remain throughout the history of the French monarchy down to the 1789 Revolution, helped by the more than usual longevity of most of the reigning monarchs.

If, then, the Carolingians wished to set aside the Merovingian royal dynasty, a supernatural sanction for the innovation would have to be found. Pepin, the Carolin-

gian aspirant, found such a sanction in the approval of
the Papacy, symbolized by his own anointing as King
of the Franks by Pope Stephen III in 754. A former Pope,
Zacharias, had remarked in reply to a preliminary sound-
ing of opinion by Pepin : 'It was better to call that man
King who has [royal] authority in practice, rather than
the man who remained [as King], though without royal
authority.' The axis thus set up between Pope and Emperor was backed up in writing at about the same time
by the strange forgery (accepted as genuine until the
fifteenth century) known as the Donation of Constantine, which purported to be a grant of rule over Rome
and Italy to the Papacy by the Emperor Constantine.
The title of 'Patrician of the Romans' granted to Pepin
by Stephen at the anointing ceremony is another pointer
to the diplomatic motives of the Papacy.

Papal diplomacy then, as usual in the Middle Ages,
was conditioned by the situation in Italy. Ever since
the time of Gregory the Great the Papacy, progressively
robbed of Byzantine help, had been under constant pressure from the Lombards, the latest in the series of Germanic invaders of the peninsula. A loose federation of
tribes which only with difficulty accepted the principle
of permanent royal government, the Lombards had been
as aggressive towards the Papacy after their conversion
to Catholicism in the late seventh century as they had
been during the first hundred Arian years of their occupation. It was natural that the Papacy should look over
the Alps to the Frankish realms as a possible champion
against the Lombard menace.

Pepin proved willing and quick to undertake this role.
After his anointing he brought the Pope back over the
Alps and forced the Lombards into submission. Less
than twenty years later, in 774, Pepin's son Charlemagne
extinguished the Lombard realm altogether and annexed

its territories to his own. A forcible reunification of Western Europe was beginning to take place for the first time since the fall of Rome.

It was none too soon. Before the Carolingian successes it might have seemed that Christian Western Europe was destined to collapse before exterior forces too great for it to cope with. Up from Spain were pushing the conquering Arabs, whose naval power also dominated the Western Mediterranean. Western Christendom's eastern frontiers in Central Europe were either blocked by pagan Saxons in the Elbe area or battered by the formidable Avars in the Danube plain. To an impartial observer it might have seemed that Christian civilization would have to rely for its preservation on Greek Byzantium, whose riches and culture were far in advance of any of the crude Christian barbaric realms of the West.

All this was changed by the three great Carolingian rulers, Charles Martel (719–41), Pepin (741–68) and Charlemagne (768–814). Charles Martel, though content to remain Mayor of the Palace, won what was perhaps the dynasty's most important battle by defeating the Arabs at Tours, in 732, so, as it turned out, removing the chance of a dangerous Moslem penetration into the rest of the Christian West. In the days of Charles Martel there were also the beginnings of expansion eastwards with an advance into the Saxon pagan hinterland beyond the Northern Rhine. Christian missionary enterprise smoothed the way for Frankish arms and in St Boniface the infant German Church received its first administrator of genius and finally its first famous martyr. The Merovingians had already extended Frankish territory deep into Southern Germany and the conquest of the Avars by Charlemagne rounded off control of the Danube valley and made it inevitable that Central Europe would fall within the cultural orbit of Latin

Christendom. The coping-stone to possession of the West was again possession of Italy itself and particularly Rome and the way was now open for revival in theory of the Western Empire.

On Christmas Day, 800, Pope Leo III crowned Charlemagne as Emperor at Rome. There is still diversity of opinion as to what the ceremony, which may have been a surprise to Charlemagne himself, actually meant. But clearly the ritual was intended to symbolize the conveyance to the Frankish King of some kind of governing authority over Latin Christendom, and the fact that the Papacy was the agent of this conveyance indicated the religious character of the new Imperial authority. One of Charlemagne's favourite books was Augustine's *City of God* and it seems clear that the ideal of 'political Augustinism' received its first significant expression in the Carolingian age. After Charlemagne's death the ideal persisted even among the disappointments of the collapse of his heritage, Agobard of Lyons putting it in its most forthright form :

It would be pleasing to Almighty God that under one single most pious king, all men should be governed by one single law; that would be of great utility for the harmony of the City of God and justice among the nations.

Beyond the ideological imperial façade lay the reality of temporary Frankish military superiority over all rivals. How was it achieved ?

First and foremost it seems that the Carolingian military ascendancy was due to the most highly efficient deployment of the cavalry arm so far to be seen in the Christian era. This in its turn, it seems, was a corollary of the spread to the West of the use of the complete foot-stirrup, an arrival from Central Asia about the beginning of the eighth century. The new invention en-

abled the armed horseman to keep a securer seat on his
mount than had been possible hitherto and hence allowed him to use heavier armour and weapons. The
protective long shield and the heavy lance were the
most striking instances of the latter and they were to
become the standard battle equipment for most of the
Middle Ages.

Obviously this equipment would be considerably expensive and this would mean that the old reliance on in-
fantry, so central to the Graeco-Roman conception of
warfare, would never be entirely done away with. But
the major emphasis was now inevitably to shift to the
provision of an adequate amount of cavalry, and this
meant that the comparatively small elite of trained
heavily armed soldiers would become the nucleus and
decisive kernel of any ambitious war-leader. How
could the necessary expense for creating and preserving
such forces be met in an age where public taxation was
almost unknown? The obvious solution was to link the
expense of the new military requirements with the only
reliable source of wealth – ownership of land. Charles
Martel, whose victory at Tours was the first great demonstration of the strength of the new weapon, showed the
way by his ruthless seizure of Church lands for distribution among his subordinate warriors in return for
provision by them of the new military requirements.
The combination of military allegiance with guaranteed
ownership of land as its collateral, a combination which
forms the essence of what is usually defined as 'feudalism', thus owes its origin to the Carolingian period,
while it is also true that the third characteristic of feudal
organization, the power of administering law locally,
was awarded by Charlemagne to the new military and
landowning class in the person of his 'counts'. The
new pattern of human relationships on the land which

the new proto-feudal conditions created was backed up by a remarkable series of changes in food production which amounted to an agricultural revolution. But this will be reserved for discussion in the next chapter.

In the trading and commercial spheres the spell of Pirenne is gradually being broken and we are coming to look at the Carolingian era as an epoch not of decline but of the burgeoning of new economic life. The virtual abandonment of gold as the basic unit of currency was an act of enlightened realism such as might be envied by many modern statesmen; it cleared the decks for the creation of a practically controllable currency based on silver which was to hold the field everywhere in Western Europe until Napoleon and still survives today in the sterling areas. Charlemagne also perceived the economic necessity for the prevention of inflation by keeping the monopoly of minting coinage in the hands of the central authority, though this *sine qua non* of economic policy had escaped the notice of his Merovingian predecessors, so belauded by Pirenne, as it was to be disregarded by his more incompetent Carolingian successors.

To ascribe the revival of town life as the Middle Ages was to know it to the age of Charlemagne might seem to be going too far. Certainly it would be ludicrous to maintain that in the overwhelmingly agricultural economy which was Carolingian Europe the town in the sense of a financial and commercial emporium had any real existence. Nevertheless it does seem that in Carolingian times the Western European towns, mostly direct continuations of Roman predecessors on the same sites, were making a limited revival as centres of market exchange. Legislation throughout the Carolingian period on fair prices for the produce sold at such market centres suggests that the town was already re-emerging as a fundamental economic unit.

The same atmosphere of genuine, if limited, revival is to be found when one turns to the ecclesiastical and intellectual life of the age (the two, as in most of the Middle Ages, go together). Charlemagne, who took his duties as monarch of a Christian society very seriously, was deeply concerned with the problem of reforming a clerical body which in many parts of his realms had grown ignorant as well as corrupt. The secular clergy as always were the problem. The unit of ecclesiastical life in a predominantly agricultural society was coming to be the parish, an essentially Germanic cell of Church life, as contrasted with the Roman pattern of administration based on the urban centre of the diocese. The parishes could only exist economically with the support of the relevant local landowner, who became known as the 'patron' of the 'living', with the right of appointment of its clerical incumbent. During the Merovingian times establishments for the training and education of the secular clergy had been at a premium and Charlemagne was forced to enlist the help of monastic agencies in his task of moral and intellectual elevation of the Frankish Church.

Charlemagne's age saw the crystallization of the Benedictine Rule under the auspices of Benedict of Aniane; the oldest surviving manuscript of St Benedict's compilation dates indeed from this period. In the Carolingian age the great Benedictine monasteries such as St Gall and Reichenau in Germany and Fleury and St Denis in France were to become great storehouses of learning, where classical manuscripts which would otherwise have been lost were preserved and copied. To assist in the formulation of a common intellectual medium the famous Carolingian script was evolved; this was to occupy a position of no small importance in the intellectual technology of medieval Europe. Though suffering an eclipse in favour of the more complicated shorthand 'Gothic' script in the later Middle Ages, the Carolingian script was to be taken up at the Renaissance by the early printers and hence was to form the main permanently recorded method of transmitting ideas down to modern times.

The monastic educational institutions in theory were confined to youths embarking on the monastic novitiate; in practice many monasteries seem to have also given instruction to youthful laity, though the secondary status of the latter was often emphasized by assigning them a separate place of residence, sometimes even outside the monastic walls. The Carolingian monarchs, however, seem to have wished to loosen the dependence of education on exclusively monastic *milieux* by encouraging the foundation of secular educational institutions, even though the teaching personnel of such institutions might inevitably continue to be monastic. The 'Palace Schools' of the Carolingians originated as a development from a previous educational institution of the Court, aimed at imparting to young warriors and courtiers the responsibilities of their status. Charles Martel took the initiative in broadening the intellectual basis of these establishments, and Charlemagne brought over Alcuin of York, the greatest scholar of the age, to act as master over the Palace School. Later still, in the ninth century, the bishops of the Frankish realm made attempts with varying degrees of permanence to set up similar schools in association with their cathedrals. The day of these cathedral schools had not yet fully come, but when it did they were to become the ancestors of the European universities.

What sort of subjects were studied by the palace and cathedral schools? An enactment by a Roman episcopal synod in 826 gives a good contemporary description:

. . . in all bishoprics and the parishes subordinated to them, and elsewhere that it may be necessary, careful and diligent measures shall be taken to appoint teachers and learned persons who, being conversant with letters, the liberal arts, and sacred theology, are regularly to teach these subjects, because in them above all the divine ordinances are made clear and manifest.[7]

The emphasis on ecclesiastical learning is understandable in view of the primary function of the schools as educators of a reformed clergy. Scripture formed the staple of study, but it presented many problems of interpretation, and the Carolingian teachers were obviously unable to meet such problems with historically critical methods. Instead, a heavy recourse was made to allegory, already applied to the Biblical narratives in immediate pre-Christian times by the Jewish scholar, Philo of Alexandria, while the same method had been taken up by the Alexandrian school of Christian exegetes in the second and third centuries to make the Bible more understandable and perhaps more palatable to new converts from a Greek cultural background. The concepts of symbolism and allegory as the appropriate means for reinterpreting otherwise unacceptable authoritative texts and giving them a deeper esoteric significance were already current in non-Christian sources in the later Roman Empire, particularly among Neo-Platonist philosophical circles, for whom systems of ever more elaborate correspondences ran through every corner of the universe.

Augustine's system of allegorical interpretation, which was to become standard for the early Middle Ages, was rather more sober. Augustine in fact advised adherence to the literal interpretation of Scripture

7. Translation by M. L. W. Laistner, *Thought and Letters in Western Europe, A.D. 500–900*, p. 208.

whenever possible. Only when a literal interpretation would be clearly in error should resort be made to allegory. The medieval monastic tradition, which followed this Augustinian technique of interpretation, was ready to apply it even to profane writers. Thus Ovid, despite his scurrilities, was used as a vehicle of philosophic wisdom. This technique of benign interpretation was not deliberately disingenuous. It was based on a conviction that all truth was one and therefore could not be self-contradictory; if apparent discrepancies existed, they could be resolved by exploration below the surface meaning.

Such was what might be described as the strategy of interpretation of recognized authorities. The tactics of interpretation were borrowed largely from the method set forward by Macrobius, an early fifth-century commentator on the so-called *Dream of Scipio*, the last surviving fragment of Cicero's dialogue *The Republic*. Macrobius' careful commentary on the Ciceronian text was taken as a pattern by future medieval commentators on any text, while the subject matter of the *Dream*, spiritual and other-worldly even though pagan, appealed strongly to the transcendental orientation of early medieval Christianity, with its tendency towards asceticism and 'contempt of the world'. Cicero the statesman and man of affairs was unknown and he became instead the archetype of the contemplative sage-philosopher.

The other significant element in the quotation from the bishops of 826 is the mention of 'the liberal arts'. The idea of this basis for the technique and matter of knowledge goes back to the Greek tradition of rhetorical education exemplified by Isocrates, though it was also widened to include the more 'scientific' studies commended by Plato. By the time of Augustine the liberal arts had become standardized as seven in number; medicine and law (which had found their way into some Graeco-Roman lists) had been eliminated as being too technical. Augustine's list included grammar, logic, rhetoric, music, geometry and philosophy. The standard form of the liberal arts was, however, derived from the strange allegorical work of an African contemporary of Augustine, Martianus Capella, whose *Marriage of Mercury and Philology* introduced the seven arts as bridesmaids at the wedding in question. Capella substituted astronomy for Augustine's 'philosophy' and this was later adopted also by Cassiodorus, a contemporary of Boethius in the sixth century. The Capella–Cassiodorus classification became definitive in the Carolingian age itself. The Carolingian scholars split the seven arts into lower and higher subdivisions, the *trivium* (grammar, dialectic, rhetoric) dealing with the technique of correct thought and expression, and the *quadrivium* (arithmetic, geometry, astronomy and music) dealing with the subject matter of accurate knowledge. Thereafter the seven arts became an indispensable basis for any form of early medieval education. They were to remain so until the Renaissance.

Such was the curriculum which became basic during the Carolingian period. On its foundations a respectable philosophical edifice began to be laid. As usual in the West, problems of practical interest, ethical behaviour, the fate of the individual soul, were the primary staple of discussion. A furious controversy on predestination raged throughout the middle of the ninth century, the central protagonist being the Benedictine Gottschalk, whose own unhappy career (he had been entered into the monastic life as a child and forced to unwilling continuance in it as an adult) led him to elaborate a gloomily exaggerated version of Augustine's doctrine. Gottschalk's theory of double predestination (that is, that each individual was destined either to damnation or grace) aroused violent opposition from more moderate theologians, who accused him of completely destroying individual freedom; the more liberal arguments were backed by illiberal action on the part of Gottschalk's abbot, Rabanus Maurus, who imprisoned the erring monk in solitary confinement for the rest of his life. In prison Gottschalk, who was an artist as well as a theological polemicist, wrote one of the most moving of medieval Latin poems to bewail his lot –

> Oh why bid me, little one,
> Oh why order, little son,
> Me to sing a cheering song
> When I've been an exile long,
> Far beyond the sea?
> To sing why order me?[8]

The predestination controversy which was so fatal for Gottschalk is an example of the absorbing interest in the problems of personal status and behaviour which so preoccupied Western Christendom as compared with its Greek counterpart. The figure of John Scotus Eriugena, contemporary and opponent of Gottschalk, marked an attempt, isolated but influential, to combine the resources of Greek metaphysical theology with the more practical Latin genius. Perhaps only an Irishman would have attempted such a task and indeed there is much in John's system which reminds us of the fantastic profundity which had set Celtic Christianity apart from the remainder of Western Christendom since the fifth century. A Christianity congenial to reason and imagination alike (and nowhere else was their conjuncture so fruitfully achieved), where asceticism and hu-

8. Author's translation.

manism managed to coexist without tension, Irish Christianity had met in the conversion of Anglo-Saxon England with the institutional organization of Rome; the marriage of the two traditions had made eighth-century England the intellectual leader of Western Europe. Significantly enough it was to Alcuin of York that Charlemagne had turned to guide the Frankish attempt at educational reform.

Eriugena's knowledge of Greek, unique for his time, enabled him to use intellectual material previously unavailable to the West. His dispute with Gottschalk had turned his mind in the direction of vindicating the benignity of God's ways to Man and his knowledge of the sixth-century Greek mystical writer whose writings were erroneously attributed to Dionysius the Areopagite, a disciple of St Paul mentioned in the Acts of the Apostles, turned Eriugena's speculation in a novel direction. The Pseudo-Dionysius had put into Christian terms the Neo-Platonist conception of the cosmos as a vast hierarchical system, ultimately derivative from a God who could not be fully grasped by reason; this system found within it a place for every grade of life, however lowly; the system was one of relationship through intermediaries up the whole ladder of existence, 'the Great Chain of Being', as this concept has been called by the modern historian of ideas, A. O. Lovejoy. The principal Greek commentator on the Pseudo-Dionysius, Maximus the Confessor, made the Dionysian system more explicitly Christian by linking it more closely with the Christian pattern of redemption and salvation, but it was left for Eriugena, who translated both writers into Latin, to take the process to its supreme conclusion in his own original speculation.

Eriugena's *De Divisione Naturae* (The Division of Nature) has been well described by Étienne Gilson as 'that

immense metaphysical and theological epic'[9] and there
is indeed a certain compelling dramatic quality in Eriugena's presentation of the universe as an arena of multi-
farious activity which is ultimately reducible to pure
thought and in which every manifestation of life is
seen as in some sense a manifestation of God. Hierarchy in active development is how Eriugena sees the
whole of universal being; hence every legitimate part of
this hierarchy is both statically serene and yet at the
same time tensely expectant. It is serene because it holds
to its appropriate place in the hierarchical chain; it is
expectant because it knows that this hierarchical division will be in the end subsumed in the return of all
things to direct union with God – Eriugena's version of
the Last Judgement. As in most optimistic philosophies
of the universe, the problem of evil was the snag in
Eriugena's system. While admitting that evil blinded
fallen Man to the realities of Divine truth, and while insisting with the Dionysian school that this meant that
Man needed supernatural help to remove this obstacle
to reason, Eriugena held that in the end evil would, as a
purely negative force, cease to have any real existence.
He went as far as to argue that eternal damnation was
merely the *memory* of evil in the mind of the damned.
Hell for him, like Mexico for Graham Greene, was a
state of mind.

Eriugena was as much a disciple of Augustine as of
Dionysius and it was doubtless from Augustine that his
conception of love as the motive force behind this
grandiose cosmic movement was derived. Eriugena sees
the gratuitous love of God, the originally unknowable
Absolute Being, for a world which He has called into
Being out of nothing, as the deep impetus below all uni-

9. *History of Christian Philosophy in the Middle Ages*, 1955,
p. 127.

versal life; the love of the different parts of the universe, the different ranks of its hierarchy, for each other, are just innumerable expressions of the ultimate Divine Love which sustains them all. Just as love inspired God's outgoing movement towards created Being, so the return quest for God by created Being is also inspired by love. The Eriugenian universe is certainly an interlocking, institutional hierarchy; but it is also a system of specific, reciprocal, sometimes personal relationship.

Eriugena's philosophical theology was too near the bone of pantheism to make him an acceptable authority for the Western Church. Hence he remains the great odd man out among medieval philosophers. In later centuries disciples of his works and the works themselves were condemned as heretical, and the Dionysian writings which he had introduced to the West did not exercise much influence, even on mystical theology, until after the more accurate translation by Sarrazin in the thirteenth century. Yet, for all the West's cold-shouldering of him, it may not be fanciful to suggest that Eriugena's philosophy aptly symbolizes the unique flavour which distinguishes medieval Latin Christianity.

Early Christianity, as we have seen, had been preoccupied with the expectation of the apocalyptic consummation of the world. Augustine had liberated it from the identification of the end of all things with the fall of the Roman Empire, but even after him, and perhaps partly because of his pessimistic view of worldly authority, Christian society had tended to regard the Last Day as just around the corner and had not therefore been able to take much interest in the task of permanent organization of a civilization to succeed that of Rome. If there was any such limited interest it was linked to the long-standing illusion that Rome had not really died, that it was merely waiting to be revived. This kind of political ghost-raising had lain behind the crowning of Charlemagne as Emperor.

But the Carolingian age had marked the first movement in another direction – the temporal institutionalization of Christianity itself as a framework for civilization in the same sense that the Graeco-Roman culture had been for the classical world. With Charlemagne a single Christian ruler had at last emerged over most of the Western world; unity in belief and unity in social structure were associated for the first time in Christian history. Charlemagne's legal *Capitularies* mark the intention to direct an emergent social order on a distinctively Christian basis and this ideal would persist in the breach or the observance throughout all medieval history. In this task of reclamation of society for Christianity, the sense of the imminence of the End of the World and the consequent futility of any earthly effort was not indeed forgotten but it did tend to sink into a background acknowledged but not reflected upon. Only in moments of catastrophe and extreme tension, or among the extreme fringes of rebellion against existing organized society, did the eschatalogical aspect of Christianity regain its full urgency.

Meanwhile the qualified acceptance of social responsibility by Christianity, which it never repudiated after Charlemagne, gave rise to a new tension between Christianity's own unique 'personalist' emphasis (an emphasis which, we have suggested, was one of the reasons for its success) and the greater institutionalization which would be necessary for the effective development of a Christian society. This tension would only be resolvable if the individual, while still safeguarding his sense of personal uniqueness, could at the same time accept a status within the institutional framework. The bonds of personal contract and personal delegation which are the basis of the proto-feudalism of the Carolingian period as well as of the more developed feudalism of later times were the medieval answer to a perennial Christian problem. And the intellectual system of John Scotus Eriugena, with its vision of a universe of an institutionally articulated hierarchy motivated by the personal love circulating between its different members, is a sublimation, at once beautiful and profound, of this answer.

By the time of Charlemagne Christianity had decided not to kill time but to use it. It was now also committed to the bold experiment of attempting to realize the values of a personally orientated religion through the medium of a communally orientated temporal society. The formidable difficulties of this apparently paradoxical enterprise will form the theme of the rest of this book.

4

LORDS, LADIES, LAND AND PEOPLE

THE agrarian history of the Middle Ages presents a somewhat paradoxical duality of aspect. On the one hand, it can be viewed as the steady growth of the great seigneurial domain, that complex of economic, legal, political and military privileges to which the umbrella word 'feudal' has been attached as a label. But on the other hand it has been more and more realized in recent years that the same period marked an equally steady growth of prosperity and cohesion among smaller non-seigneurial peasant proprietors, and that this growth of the peasantry, individually and communally, was a factor which seigneurial authority constantly had to reckon with.

The gradual decline of slavery as a viable vehicle of economic organization is the feature which differentiates most clearly the classical Roman from the early medieval worlds. The Roman slave lived herded with his fellows in great barrack-like communal dwellings; he had no private property, no family life. The serf of the early Middle Ages, on the other hand, had acquired his own small private dwelling, his own small subsistence plot of land and a family to which he could hand on these possessions. How did the change come about?

One reason was that the cessation of the Roman wars of conquest meant the cessation of the means of replenishing slave labour, given the fact that the inability of the slave to form a family relationship resulted in the impossibility of replacing passing slave generations by natural reproduction. A further reason was that, as the economic situation of the Empire worsened, it became more and more onerous for slave-owners to face the burden of expenditure on the upkeep of vast numbers of slaves. It became more economical to turn the slave into an hereditary tenant on the lord's estate, with certain stipulated services. Economics rather than ethics freed the slaves.

Slaves were not the only Roman class who were metamorphosed by events into the composition of the medieval serf. From the early days of the Empire the practice had been adopted of settling on smallholdings a type of free peasantry, very often ex-soldiers, who were now given a long-desired share in the land as a reward for their services. These *coloni* (literally 'cultivators') were technically free but by the time of the later Empire they were brought within the scope of the general vocational 'freezing' which Emperors such as Diocletian and Constantine considered to be essential to their economic policy. The *coloni* were now bound to stay on their plots of ground, generation after generation 'to eternity', as one of the Imperial enactments put it. Technically as freemen their master was the Imperial authority alone but as time went on we find that the function of tax-collecting from the *coloni* is progressively handed over to the great landowners of the district. By the third century the Imperial laws were taking it for granted that the typical *colonus* would be working on the estate of a *dominus* ('lord'). By the second half of the same century whole villages had fallen under the personal patronage of a *dominus*. Legislation aiming at punishing the flight of a *colonus* from his hereditary land shows the oppressive conditions which must have been brought to many. Yet the growth of villages which can be traced at this period shows that some of the *coloni* must have found the new arrangements to be on balance advantageous. The growth in the practice of commendation (entrusting oneself to the protection of an important noble in return for entrance into a tenant relationship) was another example of a proto-feudalism which, initially anyway, was in the interest of both parties.

Thus by the time of the barbarian invasion a transformation of agrarian structure in the direction of a contractual relationship between landed aristocrat and peasant tenant was already taking place. Did the German newcomers bring any radical changes to the picture?

It is extremely difficult to establish incontrovertible facts about the primitive economic organization of the German tribes before their appearance in the Roman Empire. The principal sources of written information are the first-century Latin writers Tacitus and Pliny the Younger. Tacitus' *Germania* has been suspected by some modern critics of being a disguised reforming tract for the Roman times rather than a factual account of Teutonic conditions; certainly it seems absurd to read into Tacitus, as some romantically minded nineteenth-century German historians did, an alleged primitive community of land ownership. As far as we can gather from Tacitus' enigmatic remarks, it seems that he intended to present the Germans of his time as owning land individually and with frequent mutually agreed alternations of arable land, aristocrats having priority of choice. But this is as much as we can say. Tacitus intends above all to depict a society which places the accent on the warrior rather than the cultivator. As he says: 'He [the German] thinks it spiritless and slack to gain by

sweat what he can buy with blood.'[1] Tacitus' picture of
the warrior band of youths who surround the German
chief and who regard it as dishonour to survive him in
battle has a stamp of authenticity, particularly when
placed in relation to late developments of classical feudal
ideals, and it is hard to believe that this section of his
book is quite out of touch with reality.

By the time the Germans impinge in force on Rome
they have already undergone a transformation of social
structure as compared with the picture given by Tacitus. Relevant documentation is more abundant for the
Visigoths on the eve of their conversion to Arian Christianity by Ulfila and his associates in the later fourth
century, and just before their mass migration across the
existing Imperial frontiers (they had in fact been in actual occupation of the former Roman province of
Dacia, the present Rumania, since the third century).
This documentation has been worked into an admir-
able synthesis by E. A. Thompson particularly in his
examination of *The Passion of St Saba*, one of the early
Christian martyrs among the Visigoths. This fourth-
century document was intended primarily as hagio-
graphy, but it also provides much valuable information
on social conditions. As compared with the situation
presented by Tacitus, Visigothic society gives the im-
pression of a state of affairs where tribal chieftainship
has little more than a wartime significance and where
real economic, political and military authority is falling into the hands of a comparatively small number of
aristocrats with their retinues of fighting men. It also
seems clear that the Visigothic villages are at any rate
in theory subject to the wishes of the great men, though
a village assembly seems, on the evidence of the *Passion*,

1. Tacitus, *On Britain and Germany*, translation by H.
Mattingly, Penguin Classics, p. 113.

to have been able in practice to apply a brake to decisions of the nobles. If this pattern was prevalent in other German tribes (and we have no real reason to suppose that the Visigoths were exceptional) it means that the Germanic invaders of the Empire were not hardy freemen of the Teutonic forests, but rather men to whom an already clear distinction between nobility and commoner would be familiar enough to enable the newcomers to dovetail with comparative ease into the structure of proto-feudal relations which was taking shape in the later Empire.

By the time of the Carolingian Empire the dual relationship between lord and peasant to which both Roman and German society had been moving had crystallized into a definite pattern. The two institutions of the *villa* (the residence of the lord) and the *manse* (residence of the serf) were the symbols of this pattern. Each was hereditary and each was safeguarded against a breach of the compact by which each benefited. The tenant received security, the estate-owner services in kind, such as help with the harvest and a periodical number of days of work, without which the continuance of the estate's economic life would hardly have been viable.

The most detailed source of information about the great Carolingian estates is the so-called *Polyptyque* of Irminon, dating from the first quarter of the ninth century. Irminon was Abbot of Saint Germain-des-Prés near Paris and this reminds us of the important part which the great Benedictine monasteries had come to play in the economic life of Western Europe. Founded by a refugee from Roman corruption, St Benedict, in the early sixth century, the Benedictine Order originally envisaged the scanty material needs of the monks as being met by their own self-help. The enlargement of cultivable land and the clearing of forest areas owed much to the labours of the monks, but the enlargement of their estates through extensive gifts from the laity in the years between the sixth and eighth centuries transformed the abbeys into great landowning institutions with tenants and serfs on the pattern of secular lordships. The monasteries seem to have proceeded further than the secular landowners in doing away with collective work obligations for their tenants and giving the latter certain prescribed individual tasks.

The transformation of the half-seigneurial, half-communal system into full-fledged feudalism seems to have been due primarily to military and political responsibilities which were either conferred or assumed by the lords. We have already suggested that the ultimate source of these responsibilities lay in the military and political requirements of the Carolingian monarchs, which joined hands with the long process of formation of personal bodyguards which had grown up among the German ruling classes, and which also existed in Roman Imperial conditions. Naturally the Carolingians did not intend the process of grants of this feudal character to outstrip the surveillance of royal authority, but the general breakdown of central government, particularly in France, after Charlemagne, made it inevitable that privileges granted by the monarchy should be appropriated as the hereditary prerogatives of autonomous chieftains. The medieval baron came into existence.

The word 'Baro' (its original form) takes us right into the heart of the complex of custom which made up feudalism. 'Baro' was the new medieval Latin word coined for 'man' (considered as an individual) and the relationship of one fighting man to another was at the basis of the feudal contract. The entering into feudal subordination to a lord (the state of 'vassalage') was associated with the ceremony of homage, in which the vassal-to-be knelt before his prospective lord, placed his hands between the lord's and uttered the simple but binding words: 'I am your man.' By this utterance and the accompanying ritual the vassal assumed the obligation of providing the lord with military assistance when required and attending the lord's court at stated times for judicial, administrative and ceremonial purposes. Towards the end of the eleventh century money, now returning into wider circulation, entered the feudal compact, and we find the emergence of the four stand-ard feudal taxes or 'aids': for the lord's ransoming when prisoner; for the expenses of knighting his eldest son; for the expenses of marrying his eldest daughter; and to enable the lord himself to buy more land. As time went on the provision of military service by the vassal was itself commuted for a cash payment which would enable the lord to buy troops to his own liking.

In return for these obligations the vassal was given a piece of land sufficient to provide him with the necessi-ties of life for himself, his family, and the retainers needed to satisfy his own and his lord's military re-quirements. This land was designated as a 'fief'. 'Fief' was an odd Gallic word which originally meant a piece of movable property. Later it extended its meaning to include any sort of property; and finally it became as-sociated exclusively with the concept of property handed over as the result of the contract between lord and vassal. The German equivalent *Lehn* ('loan') expres-sed rather more clearly the original conception that the feudal grant of land was in theory a temporary trans-action, limited to the lifetime of the participants.

The natural human tendency to wish to make provi-sion for one's descendants frustrated in due course the

concept of the fief as a temporary grant for one lifetime only. Towards the second half of the ninth century
hereditary succession had become the rule in France,
the classic country of feudalism. The ceremony of homage for each succeeding incumbent of the fief still remained as symbolical of the theoretical right of the
overlord to dispose of the land as he wished; but in
practice hereditary succession of the eldest son came to
be regarded as automatic. The rule of primogeniture
was one of feudalism's most significant legacies to the
European tradition of law. In itself it benefited both
vassal and lord; to the former it meant a reasonable
security of tenure; to the latter it was convenient as a
means to prevent the break-up of economic and military
resources which might be needed in the future. The only
people who suffered from the arrangement were cadet
branches of the feudal families, who were now debarred
from any share in the land. It is to this fact that we can
ascribe the great wave of Norman-French emigration to
conquer lands overseas, as exemplified in the conquests
of Italy and Sicily, England, and the crusading movement in the Middle East. The case of the seven sons of a
Norman knight, Tancred de Hauteville, is a most famous
example. These in turn, except the firstborn, were dis-
patched by their father to seek their fortunes in Southern Italy. Undaunted by Saracens, Byzantines, Lombards
and the Pope, the redoubtable family ended by establishing a kingdom over the whole of the Italian South.

There was nothing to prevent a vassal from setting
up as an overlord himself by entering into a feudal
relationship, but this time receiving homage instead of
giving it. Thus a feudal pyramid began to be set up,
which threatened to lead to a minute subdivision of
authority and proprietorship. One way out of the difficulty which was tried was the system of 'liege homage',

by which one particular Lord was recognized to have first claim on the services of vassals in case of doubt or conflict. France was once more the origin and classic centre of this new type of feudal relationship. But in its turn it broke down. The paradoxical procedure of permitting liege homage to more than one lord defeated the original purpose of the whole exercise. It was only in England, where William the Conqueror and his successors could call in the additional buttress of strong royal authority, that liege homage assumed any enduring significance.

It would be a mistake to imagine that the feudal system was invariable from country to country. This was not the case. It was strongest in impact on France, the country of its origin. This was probably because here royal authority had become weakest and hence had had to allow greater fragmentation of authority. In Germany, by contrast, the monarchy retained greater centralizing vitality in the earlier part of the medieval period while the continuance of the existence of the great tribal duchies (Saxony, Franconia, Bavaria, Swabia, Lorraine) also held up the growth of feudal relationships. We shall see in a later chapter that paradoxically the greater strength of feudalism in France paved the way for a revival of the monarchy to an extent impossible for Germany. England would presumably have gone the same way as Germany but for the brutal but levelling process of the Norman Conquest, which produced a monarchy which led the field in exploiting the centralizing potentialities in the feudal relationship.

Nor would it be true to say that the feudal system prevailed everywhere at the expense of the free proprietors. A considerable number of middling or small landowners, holding their possessions as 'allodial' (free) property, remained, especially in Germany. At the same time it is probable that these proprietors showed a marked decline in the Western lands during the ninth to thirteenth centuries. In areas newly reclaimed from forest or swamp, where the new residential settlements known as *villes neuves* ('new towns') arose, the drive towards feudalism would be less; the prize of free status was an incentive to cultivation in these difficult areas. The same would apply to areas of fresh colonization, such as the lands beyond the Elbe, where the first German *Drang nach Osten* went on from the tenth to the thirteenth centuries at the expense of the Slavs.

Manorial administration (arising from royal grants of jurisdiction to a lord) and feudal proprietorship did not always dovetail. The often scattered composition of fiefs and consequent tangle of jurisdictions meant that the tenant peasant often literally had more than one master. But by the eleventh century it would seem that the average Western European peasant was a member of a seigneurially dominated community, possibly dove-tailed into a feudal network, and that he owed a number of burdensome services to the lord in return for the latter's protection for his life and limb. Labour services, levies for use of facilities such as the lord's mill, marriage and inheritance charges – such were some of the ways by which the lord exploited the serf's dependent position. Provided he complied with these stringent restrictions, the serf occupied a position superior to that of the slave of classical antiquity in that he could inherit and transmit his own private property.

As the feudal ages wore on, the aristocratic warrior class became more stratified and exclusive. Entrance into the ranks of the great barons in the earlier centuries (ninth to eleventh) had been comparatively easy, depending chiefly on organizing ability and armed fortune. But from about the eleventh century onwards, the feudal aristocracy laid more emphasis on hereditary dignity of birth. A greater elaboration of the ritual ceremonies connected with feudal initiation reflected this increased emphasis on status. The ceremony of conferring of knighthood took its final form in the eleventh century, and it is significant that the blessing of the knight's sword and his other insignia had now become a religious rite. These ceremonies gave rise to the concept of 'chivalry' so beloved of Neo-Gothic writers, as being the code of behaviour distinguishing a knight from other men. The precepts of this code included the defence of the Church, the protection of widows and orphans, courtesy to defeated adversaries and general help to those in need. Doubtless practice fell far short of ideal in many cases, but the influence of Christianity gave Western European feudalism a tinge of ethical religious responsibility which differentiates it from other apparently similar social groupings elsewhere. The *Samurai* class of Japan, so often cited as the nearest analogy to Occidental feudalism, does not in practice appear to have extended its ethos much beyond a combination of primitive clan loyalty with a derivative and watered-down Confucianism.

Orthodox Christianity did in fact lend itself to adoption by the feudal fighting elite much more than its origins as a religion of peace would suggest. More than any other world religion, Christianity concentrated attention on its Divine Founder as a Person worthy of the utmost conceivable loyalty and service and this feeling was also the emotive force behind the feudal relationship. The two concepts of loyalty were frequently coalesced in a picture of Christ as the perfect embodiment of both; in the Anglo-Saxon *Dream of the Rood*, though this does not come from an explicitly feudal environment, we are presented with Christ as a young warrior, hastening to do combat with evil through his death on the Cross. Feudal concepts had indeed entered into Christian theological speculation on the nature of Christ's redemptive Atonement; the 'ransom' theory of the Redemption, as treated, for example, by St Anselm in his *Cur Deus Homo* at the end of the eleventh century presents Man as a rebellious vassal who has broken his oath of fealty to God, his Overlord, and illegally transferred his loyalty to another lord – the devil. The situation was only restored when Christ, the Son of God, assumed humanity, though without its felonious guilt, and was so able by His loyalty even unto death to rescue Man by taking on Himself the punishment for Man's felonious breaking of his contract. Despite the mechanical legalism of the thought behind Anselm's theory, the concept of disaster redeemed by loving loyalty is a beautiful and attractive one. Anselm himself expressed his theology in more emotive form in his 'Prayer before the Cross': 'By thee human nature, defiled by sin, finds its justification, is saved from condemnation, liberated from slavery, guilt and hell, raised from the dead.' It is re-echoed again and again in both secular and clerical expression in the feudal period.

The feudal relationship was deepened by turning it from a legal obligation into, at its best, a union of mind and heart between its participants; it is affection as well as loyalty which makes Roland in the famous *chanson* fight to the death for Charlemagne; affection as well as loyalty is responsible for the grim vendettas of the *Nibelungenlied*. At a more specifically Christian level the same personal deepening of an 'institutional' relationship is found in the affective mysticism of St Bernard of Clairvaux and the Cistercian school of mystics. For Bernard religion is an intensely personal relationship of lovers; the sense of distance between God and Man, the sense of Man's shortcomings when face to face with God, are never absent, but they are softened by the unbreakable trust and friendship which can find a focus in the Humanity of Jesus. The cult of the Divine Name with which Bernard was so deeply associated and which formed the inspiration of a hymn of the nobility of *Jesu, dulcis memoria*, was no mere magical incantation; by dwelling lovingly on the Name of the Divine Beloved, the Christian soul could feel itself in a personal contact with God impossible to achieve in the more starkly 'negative' Dionysian theology, for which God was and remained beyond comprehension, beyond definition. Christian mysticism and Christian feudalism were alike seeking to infuse the warmth of a personal relationship into what might otherwise have acquired the coldness of an exclusively legal relationship.

The cult of relics and pilgrimages was another expression of this search of the personal, though it was obviously open to superstitious abuse. At any age it appears to be a natural human tendency to seek contacts with loved or admired but no longer physically present persons by preserving and cherishing objects which have been directly or indirectly connected with them in life. So it was as a concomitant of the religious 'personalist' fervour of the feudal age that a great concentration of psychological attention on the remains of the great saints of the Christian past should take place. All over the West the shrines of the holy dead, usually associated with monasteries, became the centre of painstaking journeyings, undertaken in a spirit partly of renunciation, partly of a frantic search of personal reassurance and union with the manifestation of God's mighty Hand in the world of men.

The mingling of secular and clerical along the pilgrim roads and at the great sanctuaries found its remarkable synthesis in the epic vernacular poems of the twelfth century known as the *Chansons de Geste*. These poems, of which the *Song of Roland* is the most famous, were supposed in the nineteenth century to have been 'written-up' versions of much older half-pagan Germanic folk stories. After the researches of J. Bedier at the start of this century it is no longer possible to accept this and it now seems established that, whatever modifications may have been suggested to Bedier's analysis, its basic assertion of the close connexion between the epics and the monastic centres of the pilgrimage routes remains firm. The *Chansons de Geste* are, in fact, in obvious literary affiliation to older hagiographical vernacular poems in French, such as the *Life of Saint Alexis*, written in the same metrical form as was to be adopted by the *Chansons*. The *Chansons* also carried over into their ethos elements of deeply felt Christian belief to enter into an alliance with feudal 'heroic' concepts, an alliance which may have seemed easier to twelfth-century society than it can to us today.

We may use the *Song of Roland* as an illustration of this interaction of feudalism with Christianity. The story of this famous epic is based on a relatively unimportant historical event which occurred in 778 as an epilogue to an expedition by Charlemagne into Northern Spain against the Moorish principalities there. On his way back through the Pyrenees Charlemagne's rearguard, which may have been commanded by a certain Count Roland, was ambushed and wiped out by Basque mountaineers. Charlemagne may not have been much put out by the incident, but it was handed down in Basque tradition, which constructed its own commemorative epic of this local peasant triumph in the *Song of Altabiskar*, from which the following two verses are quoted –

What seek amid our crags these northern men?
Why have they come down here, our peace to vex?
When God the lofty cliffs between us set
He wished them to be pathless to all men!
Down crash the rocks along the mountain's length!
The foreign troops are crushed, their ranks are rent,
Their blood in torrents flows, their quivering flesh,
Their broken bones, beneath the mountain-crests
Beside the rushing streams for e'er shall rest!

They break! they flee! They, who had might and steeds,
Desert their dead upon the gory field!
Flee, mighty king with cape of scarlet, flee!
Your noble nephew, brave Roland, lies here,
Buried beneath a rock, under a tree!
Around in death's array, the dozen peers!
No doughty deeds could save their company![2]

The story of Roland's rearguard action may have
reached France through contact with Northern Spain as
a result of travel to and from the great pilgrimage shrine
of St James at Compostela, in Galicia. By the time that
the *Chansons de Geste* were being elaborated the crusading concept had taken possession of the imagination
of feudal society. The First Crusade (1096–9) had been
launched in a wave of enthusiasm for the recovery of
the greatest of all shrines – the Holy City of Jerusalem.
The great expedition, itself immortalized in a number
of *Chansons*, set up for a time a Western European kingdom of Jerusalem which led for nearly a century a precarious existence in the Middle East and served as a
textbook case of a self-consciously organized feudal
kingdom. The picture of Godfrey de Bouillon wading
through Moslem and Jewish blood at the fall of Jeru-

2. Translation by Mario Pei, quoted from *Medieval Age*, ed.
A. Flores, p. 21.

salem in 1099 to give devout thanks to God at the Holy Places is an image of the inconsistencies jostling one another in the feudal Christian ethic. The idea of a holy war to vindicate vassal disloyalty had been adumbrated in the Papacy's support of William the Conqueror's expedition to England in 1066 (William's feudal version of events being supported by the Bayeux Tapestry), while the appeal to armed force to unseat an alleged enemy of the Church had also been employed by Gregory VII against the Emperor Henry IV. But the perennial warfare against the Moslems in Spain was the clearest example of 'holy war' before the Crusades themselves.

The *Song of Roland* transforms the rearguard defeat by the Basques into a literally epic struggle against the Moslems, the 'enemy' *par excellence* for feudal tradition. Charlemagne is persuaded by the traitor Ganelon to entrust Roland and the Twelve Peers of France with the task of covering the retreat of the main army by guarding the Pass of Roncesvalles. Ganelon betrays the plan to the Moorish princes of Spain who turn up in overwhelming force and a series of bloody encounters follows, described in terms of single combats. Roland refuses to blow his horn which would summon the main army back to his assistance and does not do so until it is too late to achieve a rescue. Roland and his men are killed after feats of superhuman valour, and the task of avenging them is carried out by Charlemagne.

The figure of Roland is a fully rounded picture of the feudal hero in all his virtues and defects. His loyalty to his obligations (as he understands them) to his lord and to God is impressive, this double-edged ethos being expressed most clearly in the words put into Roland's mouth in praise of his famous sword Durendal –

Ah, Durendal, fair, hallowed and devote,
What store of relics lie in thy hilt of gold!
St Peter's tooth, St Basil's blood, it holds,
Hair of my lord St Denis, there enclosed,
Likewise a piece of Blessed Mary's robe;
To Paynim hands 'twere sin to let you go;
You should be served by Christian men alone,
Ne'er may you fall to any coward soul!
Many wide lands I conquered by your strokes
For Charles to keep whose beard is white as snow,
Whereby right rich and mighty is his throne.[3]

There is no sense of incongruity to the author of the *Song* in depicting Roland's death-dealing sword as full of holy relics. There could in fact be no better explanation of the feudal warrior's wish to personalize all his loyalties, whether to Christendom, to his lord or to his own honour. The sword itself, symbol of his knightly prowess, receives a personal farewell which would have been reserved in other cultures for a friend or a lover.

The darker side of Roland lies in his pride, expressed most clearly in his original refusal to blow his horn to secure help. This tendency to exaggerated self-reliance was condemned by both feudal and Christian ethical standards. Once more we see how the two apparently dissimilar codes merge into a single social atmosphere reflecting the moral dispositions of upper-class early medieval society.

The development of the monastic orders in early medieval Europe followed with a remarkable degree of parallelism the organizational developments of secular society itself. Monasticism in its Egyptian origins seems to have had a largely peasant personnel and may indeed

3. Translation by Dorothy L. Sayers, *The Song of Roland*, Penguin Classics, p. 141.

even be seen as part of the general peasant attempt to break free from the onerous economic burdens of the Late Empire. Something of this may still be seen in the sturdy self-help of the early Benedictine communities at Monte Cassino and elsewhere, but the *Rule of St Benedict*, with its placing of supreme power over each monastery in the hands of a lifetime abbot, is advancing towards a seigneurial structure rather like the contemporaneous evolution of agrarian administration. Benedict of Aniane's reform of the Benedictine Order in the early eighth century was undertaken as part of the Carolingian drive for religious renewal, and the oldest surviving copy of St Benedict's rule does in fact date from this period. Carolingian Benedictine monasteries included every provision for social and economic needs; and, as we have seen, before Charlemagne Benedictine abbeys were already centres of great landed estates of a proto-feudal type.

The next great innovation in monastic types was the arrival of the Cluniac reform. Cluny, founded in 909 by the Count of Aquitaine as a self-conscious centre of Church reform in an age which certainly needed it, adopted the novel system of making all daughter houses come into subjection to the mother foundation. The pattern of feudal connexion between overlord, vassals and sub-vassals finds a clear parallel in Cluniac organization, as Professor David Knowles has recently pointed out.

The great Romanesque churches of the feudal period show the same parallelism with secular counterparts. Even if a recent description of Romanesque as 'feminine space . . . bounded by masculine stone'[4] may seem somewhat fanciful, one can easily see the resemblances be-

4. F. Heer, *The Medieval World*, *1100–1350*, Mentor Books edition, 1963, p. 381.

tween the ecclesiastical architecture of the Romanesque period and the feudal castle. A church like that of the third building (early twelfth century) at Cluny, with its two naves, its great central chancel tower and its outer range of towers, would remind the spectator of the typical castle structure, also with its central tower and *don jon* and its outercircle of defensive smaller towers. The Romanesque church was indeed God's fortress as well as His dwelling, dignified by the Real Presence of God the Son (a doctrine which was now being clarified in the great Transubstantiation controversies of the eleventh century and would finally be defined at the Council of the Lateran in 1215). Within the walls of the church the fantastic decorative patterns provided a universal encyclopedia of fact and symbol covering the whole range of Christian doctrine and secular fact and fiction.

Both Christian ecclesiastical and secular feudal traditions found also substantial agreement in their attitude towards women. The feudal age was very much a man's world, as in fact had been every previous epoch in European or world recorded history; the second sex was treated by both Christian ascetic and feudal man of the world as a disturbing and mysterious phenomenon, whose influence was either to be avoided or neutralized.

The early Christian Fathers seem to have been largely influenced by the pagan Hellenistic attitude towards sexual relations. An age which knew no middle position between asceticism and libertinism and which thought of marriage primarily in economic terms could hardly be expected to have much conception of women as individual personalities in their own right, apart from their apparitions either as temptations to be eschewed or as playthings to be exploited. Most patristic writers urge abstinence from marriage as well as from illicit

sexual intercourse as the ideal course, though they are
ready to allow marriage as a legitimate second best.
Augustine, whose attitude was particularly influential,
distrusts the sexual relationship, even within marriage,
as the most obvious symbol of fallen Man's inability to
control passion by reason, though he was ready to
allow the unedifying activity as indispensable for the
procreation of children. The argument that women
were to be reprehended because their ancestress Eve had
been the direct cause of the Fall of Man was frequently
used. Tertullian's language to the ladies may be quoted
as a specimen:

Do you not know that each of you is also an Eve? ... You
are the devil's gateway, you are the unsealer of the forbidden
tree, you are the first deserter of the divine law, you are the
one who persuaded him whom the devil was too weak to attack. How easily you destroyed man, the image of God!
Because of the death which you brought upon us, even the
Son of God had to die.[5]

This concept of woman as the great seductress crops up
again and again, in varying degrees of hysteria, throughout much of medieval literature, though it was sometimes trumped by St Augustine's reminder that the In-
carnation also had occurred through a feminine medium.
Another factor to qualify the anti-feminism of the patristic and monastic tradition was St Paul's conception of
the male-female relationship as an analogy of the relationship between Christ and the Church. But, while this
certainly dignified woman's position, it still left her in a
subordinate status, which was paralleled by her position
in the early medieval social structure until the twelfth
century.

5. Translation by D. S. Bailey, *The Man-Woman Relation in
Christian Thought*, p. 64.

There was a deeper reason which seems to have exercised a great amount of influence on clerical thinking in the feudal period. This was the idea, expressed in pagan terms by Seneca and in Christian terms by St Jerome, that a permanent sexual relationship with its usual sequel of domestic responsibilities was incompatible with a life of devotion to philosophical or theological study because of its absorption of time and diversion of attention. The presumption that a family man cannot be a philosopher is found in ancient Greek sources, was stated by St Jerome with his usual classic Rabelaisian forcefulness, was taken up in early modern times by Francis Bacon and is apparently not dead today, to judge from the words, true or apocryphal, attributed to an Oxford don: 'Nothing is so inimical to academic success as a virtuous attachment.' But the supreme instance of the dilemma caused by this conception is provided by the case of Abélard and Héloïse, which has caught the attention of the centuries because of the intellectual distinction and literary articulateness of the two protagonists.

The affair was not a romantic one in the modern sense. Abélard, already a forty-year-old philosopher of fame and promise, appointed as tutor to Héloïse, an eighteen-year-old paragon of both intellect and beauty, seduced her and then offered marriage in secret. Héloïse herself was extremely reluctant to accept, on the ground that the yoke of marriage would prevent Abélard from following to its highest possible extent his philosophical vocation. 'They refused for themselves all fleshly pleasures so that they might find rest in the embraces of no lady except Philosophy.'[6] If Héloïse herself really ex-

---

6. Héloïse as reported by Abélard in his *Historia Calamitatum*. I have ventured on a translation of the last words of the sentence which I hope is justified in its novelty by the greater light which

pressed this opinion, we can find no more striking proof of the way in which even one of the most formidably intellectual women of her time had brainwashed herself into acceptance of the dominant ethos. On Abélard's insistence the marriage did in fact take place but the dilemma was solved soon afterwards by the brutal castration of Abélard by Héloïse's uncle and guardian, an event which sent Abélard back to a turbulent but distinguished philosophical career and Héloïse to a nunnery.

At first sight it might seem that the free-and-easy *amours* of the feudal nobility were poles apart from the shunning of women characteristic of the ecclesiastical tradition. In practice there was little difference of attitude, except that the feudal lord was prepared to take the chance of sleeping with his dangerous though inferior sexual opposite number rather than leave her severely alone in the manner of the conscientious cleric.

In the *Chansons de Gestes* we have a number of instances where desirable ladies throw themselves at the heads of somewhat shocked knights; the female of the species was supposed by the ethos of the *Chansons* to surpass the male in sexual desire, and this idea died hard. It would combine very readily with the more ecclesiastical idea of woman as the hardened, unscrupulous seductress.

Marriage for the feudal ethos was permissible, but no more for romantic reasons than it was for the clerical ethos. While for the clerical outlook marriage had been permissible as a safety valve for definitely unlawful lust and a vehicle for preservation of the species, for the feudal lord it was primarily a means of preserving the feudal inheritance from breaking up. In neither point of

it sheds on the author's meaning. It is hard not to believe that the writer has not in mind here a direct reference to Boethius' feminine personification of Philosophy.

view did any sense of personal love have any place.

Round about 1100 signs of tension in the feudal structure began to appear. Apart from the challenge coming from the rising urban societies, which will be discussed in a later chapter, a fissure between upper and lower echelons of the feudal pyramid was taking shape. The minor vassals and landless knights, the cadet sons of the type of the Hauteville brothers, were demanding a greater share in the fruits of the feudal establishment than the bigger magnates, barons, dukes, counts and bishops were prepared to give. In almost every Western European country a confusing shifting of loyalties and long and violent outbreaks of turbulent fighting signalized the bids of the lower members of the feudal hierarchy to carve out for themselves a place in the sun. In Italy the *vavassours* (minor vassals) of Lombardy used the excuse of conflict between the Empire and Papacy to overturn control by their feudal superiors, the bishops who deputized for the Imperial authority. Many provinces of disunited France, especially the huge southwestern duchy of Aquitaine, became the seat of petty warfare between one small castle-owner and another. Germany, exhausted by the struggle with the Papacy, saw the fortresses of robber barons shoot up to dominate its mountains and rivers, while the anarchy of Stephen's reign in England moved the Anglo-Saxon Chronicler to echo the popular complaint that God and His Saints slept.

Out of the chaos a new type of personal relationship and a new type of literature began to appear – the 'courtly love' tradition. The novelty of this was that for the first time it attempted to set male and female relationships on a basis which presupposed nothing but the freely chosen wishes of the parties themselves. The requirements of neither Church nor property played any real part. The movement and the ideas and feelings which it embodies found a centre in Southern France and the development of the Provençal vernacular of that region. The proximity to Spain has led many modern scholars to reason in favour of the influence of Moorish Arabic culture on the courtly love ethos and it is indeed true that Arabic amorous poetry of the tenth and eleventh centuries does show an approach to the conception of romantic attachment between man and woman which is the distinguishing characteristic of courtly love. In poets such as Ibn Hazm (994–1064), the Spanish Moorish thinker and poet, a detailed description of the psychological development of what we should call 'romantic love' stands far in advance of anything previously produced in Latin Christendom. It has also been noted that some of the Arabic love poets express the relationship between lover and beloved as being a servant-master relationship, even going so far as to emphasize this by addressing the female by masculine pronouns of lordship and so implying her superior status, at any rate in the world of love, to the male lover. 'To a free man,' declared the Caliph Al Hakim I of Cordoba, 'submission is good when it is in the service of love.'

The great likelihood of Arabic influence on the formation of the courtly love ethos should not blind us to the presence of influences nearer home. The age-old folk tradition of socially licensed infidelity of wife to husband at certain seasons of the year may well have served as an atavistic background for the conventional fixation of courtly love on the married woman rather than the young virgin who was to be the usual centrepiece of modern romantic story-telling (at any rate until recently!). This motif of real or symbolical adultery may also be linked with the challenge of smaller vassals or those of even lower rank to the greater aristocracy. Bernard of Ventadour, son of a servant of a minor noble and himself usually reputed as one of the greatest medieval poets, did not hesitate to address love poems to Queen Eleanor, wife of the Angevin Henry II of England, and Eleanor's own alleged *amours* did not exclude attractive lowly-born suitors. The language of feudal obligation is used on both sides of this suitor-mistress relationship; lovers exchange vows on the pattern of the feudal oath; the lover even does homage to his mistress as if she were his feudal overlord. This 'counter-feudalism', if we may so call it, is set up in self-conscious opposition to the pattern of feudal property relationships. In the new ethos the husband is condemned and, where possible, cuckolded because his relationship to his wife is that of a property-owner rather than that of a lover, ready to give his all even if unrecompensed. The husband's role is limited to that of *saboteur* of the ideal relationship between the lovers. King Mark of Cornwall occupies such a position in the famous legend of the illicit romance of Tristan and Isolde, which took its origin from this period.

At first the Provençal love poetry was content to move within the basic raw material of illicit love – frantic desire, satisfaction through subterfuge, abandonment by one or other party, complaint and possibly repentance. These stark realities of the sex war had been expressed in a particular form of Provençal lyric, the *pastourelle*, usually put into the mouth of a seduced young woman of lower birth, but the genre was taken to the highest sophisticated level by an aristocratic woman poetess of genius, Countess Beatritz de Dia –

> I'll sing, although I'm loath to make this plea,
> For he I love brought me misery,

There's no one on the earth so dear to me;
But gentleness he scorns, and courtesy.
For all my wit and charms he doesn't care.
More slighted and deceived I couldn't be
If mockery in my eyes you'd seen me bare. . . .
Dear friend, your pride has struck me with dismay.
Unjustly from my loving side you stray.
Another now has coaxing words to say,
Another smiles and welcomes you today.
Think of the kissing – dawn of our affair –
O God, absolve me from all guilt, I pray!
This parting brings me nothing but despair. . . .[7]

A new stage in the development of the courtly ethos was marked by the poetic output, small though its remains are, of Cercamon (middle twelfth century), who introduces the concept of the timidity of the lover in the presence of his beloved, proclaims his faithfulness to her despite her public rejection of him and announces that to her he owes all his culture and capacity for good. Here we have the beginnings of the idea of the loved one as a kind of goddess of intellectual as well as physical beauty, imparting by her very presence nobility and goodness of character. We also have the notion that the truth and genuineness of the lover's affection must be shown by a readiness to endure if need be all the pains of love without any requital. This complete sacrifice for love is symbolized by the public lack of recognition between the lovers necessitated by the marital conventions of the age.

The acceptance of self-sacrifice for the amatory ideal was taken to its furthest extent by poets who held that it was preferable that love should *not* be recompensed or consummated. Sordello, the Italian troubadour, implores his lady not to yield to his sensual importunities, even

7. Translation by Jack Lindsay, in *Medieval Age*, ed. A. Flores, pp. 114-15.

if she wants to. The way was now open for the complete idealization of the courtly love relationship on the style expressed most famously by Dante. The beauty of Beatrice as depicted by the Florentine poet in the *Vita Nuova* and the *Divine Comedy* is one never seen on sea or land and is in fact the supreme expression of what Plato had called the 'heavenly Venus', the embodiment of spiritual and intellectual beauty. In this rarefied attachment, which shakes itself progressively free from any hint of carnal amorous emotion, Dante can find the preamble to full Christian union with God Himself, the supreme Love –

The Love which moves the sun and the other stars.

While one strand of the courtly love tradition ended by widening by idealization the gulf between the sexes to a point almost as great as that produced by the male-centred feudal and ecclesiastical tradition, another side of the ethos preferred to explore the possibility of real friendship and psychological community between the sexes. In more mature productions of the courtly love tradition such as *Tristan and Isolde* of the German Gottfried of Strasbourg, the Provençal *Flamenca* and Chaucer's *Troilus and Criseyde*, a more intensive delineation of the relations between the lovers as two individual persons rather than two symbolic expressions of the renunciation or affirmation of sexual forces are found. Elements of the older branch of the courtly tradition are still found in these later poems, notably the fact that the heroine of all the romances is a married woman. But the focus of the author's interest in each case has shifted from the sexual game as such to the tragedy of human personal contact in its harmonies, misunderstandings and tragedies. The 'Cave of Lovers', the woodland refuge of Tristan and Isolde, is not only a love-nest for physical amorous interchange, it is also a place where the lovers tell each other tales of former lovers, sing songs and enjoy the beauties of the natural forest: 'What they did,' remarks the author, 'was entirely as they pleased, and as they felt inclined.'[8] The exigencies of the story go on to depict Tristan and Isolde agreeing, in order to minimize the chances of discovery by the pursuing King Mark, to sleep 'a good way apart from each other, just as two men might lie, not like a man and a woman. Body lay beside body in great estrangement. Moreover, Tristan had placed his naked sword between them; he lay on one side, she on the other.'[9] It was thus that King Mark found them and, after an extraordinarily acute description by the author of the King's internal hesitations, convinced himself that they were innocent.

The importance of this episode in the development of the story is obvious, but it may also serve as a symbol of the deepening and 'personalizing' of the courtly love epic. The attempt to present a possible relationship between man and woman on *all* planes can only, even for the exponents of courtly love, be sustained by presenting men and women as the same. The ascetic guilt attaching to bodily intercourse between the sexes is still strong enough to make abstention from love-making, even among lovers, seem somehow the nobler course. There is still more to the matter than this; the desire of both parties to disguise, from time to time, their relationship as one between two men is a reflection of the age-old masculine instinct that only between two men is a relation of friendship based on emotional rather than physical attachment possible. In desiring to bridge the gap between themselves and the mysterious opposite

8. *Tristan and Isolde*, translation by A. T. Hatto, Penguin Classics, p. 268. 9. ibid., p. 270.

sex, the courtly love writers could ultimately think of no better expedient than to pretend that sex differences hardly existed.

This sublimely muddled attitude was to lead to an inevitable reaction. Its most powerful expression was in the French thirteenth-century *Romance of the Rose*, a poem in two parts, written by different authors of quite different ethos. The earlier and shorter part of the *Romance*, the work of Guillaume de Lorris, is probably the classic set piece of the whole courtly love tradition. Guillaume deserts the real world for the world of allegory. His dreamer wanders in a garden and desires to approach a beautiful Rose. Helpers and enemies in the stereotyped Provençal tradition, notably 'Danger', an allegorized version of the jealous husband, aid or hinder his designs on the flower. In the event he manages to kiss the Rose once, but is then chased away from it. On this note of failure Guillaume's section of the *Rose* ends, whether deliberately or fortuitously is a matter of controversy.

The task of finishing the poem was later taken in hand by Jean de Mun, a cleric of encyclopedic learning but with no sympathy whatever for the delicacy of the courtly love ethic. Jean returns to the traditional ecclesiastical view of the unreliability of woman as a sex, but he is not for all that an upholder of asceticism. In a powerful speech put into the mouth of Nature, de Mun urges in an almost Rabelaisian fashion the frank acceptance of the joys of sex as prompted by natural instinct; so will the propagatory interests of the race be served. Lost is the individual tenderness and insight with which de Lorris had given flesh and blood to his allegorical abstractions; instead de Mun gives us a combination of bourgeois grossness, ecclesiastical conservatism and the new philosophical science of his time.

The mention of the bourgeoisie reminds us that a new cultural element was now taking the stage. Could the courtly love tradition fit into this new milieu? At first there is no doubt that the contrast between castle and town must not be over-emphasized. Gottfried of Strasbourg seems to have been a bourgeois citizen of that town; Chaucer, too, was from an originally bourgeois background, despite his later connexion with the Court. And the prince of middle-class novel writers, Boccaccio himself, included in the *Decameron* many of the elements of aristocratic *amour courtois*. But ultimately bourgeois and courtly ideals were bound to clash. The 'all for love' attitude of Tristan and Isolde, the self-renunciatory attitude of Sordello, the idealization of Dante, were all incompatible with and even incomprehensible by bourgeois society, with its realistic assessment of achievements and possibilities, its dislike of paradox as well as humbug and its unashamed interest in the goods of this world. Chaucer's artistic ventriloquism, due primarily to his own necessary straddling of both bourgeois and courtly worlds, was able to provide vivid expressions of both attitudes; the author of *Troilus and Criseyde* could also compose with relish the *Miller's Tale* and the *Reeve's Tale*.

The bourgeois attitude, however, could embody a telling criticism of the air of artificiality which haunted the courtly love ethic even at its best. Christine de Pisan, the most famous medieval female writer (late fourteenth and early fifteenth centuries) wrote a defence of her sex against de Mun's aspersions in the *Romance of the Rose*, but this did not mean that she had much more sympathy with courtly love than had de Mun. Christine rejected the *amour courtois* ethic as being itself a misapprehension of the true role of women; it was too superficial and aristocratic. Christine herself, a product of the city life of the Italian Renaissance, envisaged Woman as playing a more robust part in life than to remain the pedestalled dame or runaway wife of the courtly tradition; her age was that of the redoubtable female managers in town, court and country. The Wife of Bath is on the left wing of this regiment; Isabella of Bavaria and Margaret of Anjou occupy its political centre, while Lady Margaret Beaufort, with her college foundations, and Thomas More's daughters, who would have pleased Plato, fill its more intellectual echelons.

Perhaps the most permanent heritage of the courtly love tradition to later Europe was the concentration of interest on Woman as a being entitled to consideration in her own right. What exactly that 'own right' implied and how far it extended is perhaps not fully decided even today; but after courtly love had done its work the complacent assumptions of female worthlessness could no longer be accepted without question. A whole genre of literature in defence of Woman was current in the later medieval period. One of its most engaging examples is the Middle English poetic debate between the thrush and the nightingale (thirteenth century), in which the nightingale finally wins the day for the female cause by pointing out that the Mother of Christ was herself obviously of the feminine sex. On this the vanquished thrush declares –

> I promise by His Holy Name
> That of a wife's or maiden's fame
> No harm I'll ever say.
> I'll leave your land at once, I swear,
> And where I go, I do not care;
> I'll simply fly away.[10]

10. Modern English version by Brian Stone in *Medieval English Verse*, Penguin Classics, p. 77.

It is, of course, true that medieval religious devotion to Our Lady played its not inconsiderable part in exalting the position of women in general. One wing of the troubadour tradition addressed the Virgin Mother in terms borrowed from the more idealized conventions of their ethos, while the popular Marial legends of the Middle Ages often desert theology to present a picture incorporating almost all aspects of the revised attitude to women. Woman as the protectress and friend of the trusting servitor finds her apotheosis in the Mary of the *Golden Legend* and similar collections; St Bernard's own upbringing as a feudal vassal in the incipient courtly tradition is raised to a heavenly plane in the famous *Memorare* prayer, still unforgettable today even after its use by centuries of Catholic worshippers –

> Remember, O most gracious Virgin Mary, that
> never was it known that any who fled to thy
> protection, asked for thy help, or sought thy
> intercession, was left unaided . . .

We must now return to our focal point in this chapter – the land, and in particular to the lowest class of its inhabitants – the peasants. Relations between the feudal landed classes and the peasants were never cordial and often bitterly hostile. The hulking peasant as the noble saw him was symbolized in the figure of Goliath in literature and sculpture. Bertram de Born (*c.* 1135–*c.* 1207), the stormy petrel of the minor nobility of Aquitaine, says unblushingly –

> My heart is joyous when I see
> The cursed rich in misery
> For baiting the nobility.
> I laugh with joy to see them die,
> Twenty or thirty, knee to knee,
> Or when I see them raggedly

> Come beg for bread; and if I lie,
> Then may my mistress lie to me.
>
> For swine they're born and swine remain;
> All decency they find a strain;
> If any wealth they chance to gain,
> Then all the ways of fools they try.
> So keep their trough devoid of grain,
> Plague them with requisitions, drain
> Their pocket, and, to make them sigh,
> Let them endure the wind and rain . . .[11]

Similar sentiments can be paralleled from many poets and preachers.

Yet there is little doubt that the whole structure of feudal economy rested on the labours of the peasantry and modern scholarship has revealed the extent to which these labours and the inventions which resulted from them revolutionized the history of medieval Europe.

The great period of economic expansion which characterized the tenth to thirteenth centuries was primarily due to a population increase on a large scale and this in turn was only possible because of a number of great agricultural changes. First of all we may mention a factor about which more, though not nearly enough, is now beginning to be known – the history of medieval weather. It now seems to be clear that the Western European climate was unusually benign and temperate between 950 and 1300, and it is surely no coincidence that these dates roughly coincide with 'the age of expansion', as medieval economic historians now describe this period. Interesting literary pieces of evidence support this attempt to grasp the meteorological character of the early medieval period; images of ice, snow

11. Translation by Jack Lindsay in *Medieval Age*, ed. A. Flores, p. 118.

and cold abound in Anglo-Saxon poetry, in contrast to thirteenth-century poetry from the same English area, which incorporates a greater share of references to spring and summer and their beauties. Round 1300 the picture changed again and for the following four hundred years temperature levels declined. To complete the picture, we can add that another rise occurred from 1700 onwards and it is significant that this again co-incided with a fundamental economic revolution – the beginnings of modern industrial society.

Lynn White, Jr, the current authority on medieval economic technology, lists the main innovations in agriculture as being three in number. Firstly there was a change in the manner and use of man's weapon of the plough in cultivation. The heavier and damper soils of the North called for a plough heavier than that familiar to the classical Mediterranean countries. The new type of plough, which appears to have arrived in the West from Slav lands about the sixth century A.D., to use White's words, 'was an agricultural engine which sub-stituted animal-power for human energy and time'.[12] In particular it enabled utilization of land of the damper valley soil type, hitherto unworkable.

The new type of plough needed a greater number of oxen to draw it and was hence expensive – too expen-sive for most individual farmers. It thus led the way to greater communalization in the peasant economy and hence to more concerted planning by the village com-munity of the exploitation of the land available to it. The famous strip system of medieval agriculture may itself owe its origin to this necessity for communal col-laboration among the villagers.

The second great agricultural innovation of the early

12. Lynn White, Jr, *Medieval Technology and Social Change*, Oxford Paperback edition, p. 43.

Middle Ages was the introduction of the horse instead of the ox as the primary draught animal. This could not be possible without the previous invention of a satisfactory means of protecting the hooves of the horse, weakened by the dampness of the northern climate, against strain. The invention of the nailed horseshoe in response to this challenge was of both military and economic importance. In military matters it operated, together with the stirrup, to make the heavily armed horseman the decisive factor in warfare. The nailed horseshoe reached the West not later than the end of the ninth century and was in general use by the eleventh.

The completion of the horse's potentialities as a ploughing animal came with the adoption of a new type of harness. This substituted for the old method of attachment by the neck a much more satisfactory system of attachment to the horse's shoulders, allowing the animal greater respiratory comfort and enabling it to pull four or five times the load possible under the old method. The horse now progressively displaced the ox because it was stronger and more economical. It could produce considerably more energy than the ox could in a similar time-span and could work for longer daily periods. The horse could also be used for purposes of transport and this led to a considerable improvement of communications and greater mobility.

The third and perhaps the greatest component of the agricultural revolution was the three-field system of rotation of crops. The Graeco-Roman two-crop system (based on a winter sowing of grain in half the available land and allowing the other half to lie fallow, roles being reversed in alternate years) was replaced by the introduction of an additional spring sowing of cereals (barley, peas, beans, etc.) in a third of the land, the second third being planted in autumn with winter wheat or rye and the third section left fallow. The following year the autumn field was changed to summer crops, the spring field left fallow and the fallow field sown with winter grains. This new method may possibly have existed as early as the first century A.D. in German Rhineland districts, according to some interpretations of a passage in the *Natural History* of the Roman writer, Pliny the Elder. At all events the new system seems to have been in operation by the time of Charlemagne, though its diffusion over the different areas of Western Europe appears to have proceeded at an uneven rate.

The new crop rotation produced several spectacular results. It was both more productive and more efficient than the older system, and it also enabled the production in vastly increased quantities of protein-containing crops such as peas and beans. The increase in human vitality which the increased consumption of these crops must have brought could not but have been a major, if not the major, cause of the remarkable efflorescence of economic, intellectual and artistic activity which characterized medieval society from the tenth century onwards. A better fed people is a sure index of a culturally progressive society. As Lynn White jocularly remarks: 'In the full sense of the vernacular, the Middle Ages from the tenth century onward were full of beans.'[13]

The new techniques led to a greater self-consciousness on the part of the peasantry and a greater readiness to uphold what they regarded as their rights. In a fascinating local study Marc Bloch has outlined a prolonged legal battle in the late twelfth and early thirteenth cen-

13. *Medieval Technology and Social Change*, p. 76.

turies by the serfs of a French village to obtain freedom from their ecclesiastical monastic overlords.[14] The serfs appealed both to the Pope and the King of France and, though ultimately unsuccessful, their conduct of their case displayed such legal acumen that it is obvious that they must have disposed of sufficient wealth to purchase for themselves competent legal aid.

The peasantry in fact were on the move, both economically and geographically. The so-called 'balling' phenomenon (that is, the trend to form larger village units) was an obvious product of the greater mobility of the average peasant, who could now conveniently travel farther away from his immediate plot of land, and these larger villages were in their turn approximations to towns. They may thus have been the humble beginnings of the process which converted the Western European peasant of the Middle Ages into the town worker of today. And clearly the rising town population of the period from the tenth century onwards must have been very considerably due to a steady peasant influx. It is to the urban centres that the focal point of our survey must now turn.

14. M. Bloch, 'From the Royal Court to the Court of Rome; the suit of the serfs of Rosny-sous-bois', in *Change in Medieval Society*, ed. S. Thrupp.

5
TOWNS, TRADE, TECHNOLOGY AND THOUGHT

THE period of growth in European society which was sketched in the preceding chapter was economically an age of expansion. This period, extending roughly from the tenth to the beginning of the fourteenth centuries, was characterized by greater mobility and variety of commodities due to improvement in trade routes and general communications, the rise of professional commercial and financial classes and the efflorescence of cultural and intellectual life. The driving force behind the whole complex process was the rise in population, itself dependent most probably on the agricultural revolution mentioned in the last chapter. Trade followed the plough and helped to make good the latter's local deficiencies.

But who were the agents of this trade? Obviously many of the more well-to-do peasants would have acted as their own *entrepreneurs* and sold their own surplus produce in the city; the self-contained seigneurial estate economy was already beginning to break down. It is also clear that the representatives of the great monasteries must have carried out a certain amount of buying and selling, while at the other extreme the boundary between piracy and trade was not very closely drawn, as the career of the Vikings shows. But by the beginning of the eleventh century trade was, in fact, becoming too extensive and complex to be handled as a spare-time pursuit. The age of the professional merchant was beginning.

On this matter, as on so many other topics of medieval history, discussion on the nature of those obscure persons, the early medieval merchants, has centred on the thesis of Henri Pirenne, with its supporters and opponents. Pirenne's view of the early trade of the Middle Ages is linked up integrally with his presentation of the Islamic invasions as a complete break of continuity, economically speaking, between the Roman Imperial Mediterranean economy and the closed agriculturally based structure of Carolingian and post-Carolingian Europe. Pirenne's theory of the almost complete cessation of trade between the eighth and tenth centuries was rounded off by deducing that the resumption of trade was the work of freelance vagabonds and beggars in response to the pressure of growing population on the available agricultural land.

'It is among this crowd of foot-loose adventurers,' Pirenne argued, 'that the first adepts of trade must, without any doubt, be looked for.'[1]

Other scholars have in fact had doubts about Pirenne's theory. In particular it has been asserted that it is more plausible to suppose that the earliest traders were men with an initial modicum of capital which would enable them to take the risk of mercantile adventure. These would be more likely to come from the class of existing landowners, particularly those who held landed property in rising or reviving urban centres. Werner Sombart, whose massive studies on the origins of capitalism still provoke discussion, pointed to this class, with its exploitation of urban rentals, as the prime movers in the expansion of trade. Certainly in Italy, where there is clearer evidence than elsewhere of the drift of the landed nobility to the towns and their engagement in

1. H. Pirenne, *Medieval Cities*, English translation by F. D. Halsey, 1925, Doubleday Anchor Books edition, p. 81.

trade, Pirenne's theory would be hard to apply in its entirety and opinion is now inclined to emphasize the 'patrician' element among the early merchants rather more than Pirenne had done.

It is hard in fact to see why the two theories should not be compatible. Perhaps both Antonio and Autolycus ought each to be allotted his place in the medieval trading picture. The two elements portrayed in these Shakespearian characters certainly were united in some early merchants of the Middle Ages, notably a figure who so profoundly impressed Pirenne's own imagination – St Godric of Finchale.

Godric, an Englishman of Anglo-Saxon extraction, lived in the later eleventh and early twelfth centuries and was the subject of a hagiographical account by the monk Reginald of Durham. Though Reginald's account is obviously dominated by his wish to show Godric, even in his secular days, as worthy material for his eventual monastic vocation, it bears the stamp of verisimilitude in many of its details, and study of it sheds much light on modern controversies.

Reginald portrays Godric as wishing in early life to abandon the peasant milieu in Norfolk into which he had been born, and to seek his fortune in the wandering life of a small trader, first in his own district and later by contact with merchants in city centres. During a beachcombing expedition on the coast Godric, so his biographer declares, was miraculously saved from drowning after sparing two live porpoises but appropriating a dead one. Religion in fact, if Reginald is to be believed, seems to have been linked with economic aggrandisement as easily in Godric's mind as it was to be in those of the Reformation Puritans. Trading journeys go hand in hand with ever more elaborate pilgrimages, and Reginald complacently remarks: 'Thus aspiring ever higher and higher, and yearning upward with his whole heart, at length his great labours and cares bore much fruit of worldly gain.'[2]

Godric's commercial enterprises were eventually maritime; apparently in association 'with certain other young men who were eager for merchandise'[3] he seems to have frequented the entire North Sea area, making '. . . great profit in all his bargains, and gathered much wealth in the sweat of his brow; for he sold dear in one place the wares which he had bought elsewhere at a small price.'[4] Reginald also records a pilgrimage to Jerusalem and a return via Compostela. It must always remain a fascinating speculation whether Godric is to be identified with 'Gudric the pirate from England' who intervened in the politics of the Latin crusading kingdom of Jerusalem in 1102.[5] If he was, we may suspect that Reginald's hagiographical interest has led him to slide over this aspect of his hero's activities in the Middle East; or it might merely be that here we have a striking instance of the early conflation or confusion between merchant and pirate. Later still we find Godric reported as serving as a steward to a rich man in England and losing his job because of his rebuke to certain of his household colleagues for their thefts of cattle. At the end of it all Godric sells all his goods, distributes them to the poor and embraces the life of a hermit.

The pattern of Godric's career might well give support to both modern theories of the origin of the medieval merchant. There are admittedly many elements in God-

2. *Life of St Godric*, translation by G. G. Coulton. Quoted in *The Portable Medieval Reader*, ed. J. B. Ross and M. M. McLaughlin, New York, 1949, p. 141.

3. *Life of St Godric*, op. cit., p. 140.

4. ibid., p. 141.

5. A. L. Poole, *From Domesday Book to Magna Carta*, 1087–1216, Oxford History of England, Oxford, 1951, p. 94.

ric's freelancing activities which remind us of Pirenne's thesis; on the other hand, the emphasis on the necessity of association to obtain capital for his various enterprises would imply some truth in the arguments of Sombart and his successors. Perhaps the two may to some extent be reconciled in the generalization, which would now be accepted by most economic historians, that the merchant of the 'Age of Expansion' (to borrow M. M. Postan's terminology) was much more of a freelance than his fourteenth- and fifteenth-century successor. It is unfortunate, from the point of view of historical understanding, that documentation for the latter period is much more copious than for the Age of Expansion. This accident has misled many past historians into supposing that the *dirigisme* and economic regimentation more characteristic of the later period of depression and contraction applied to the Middle Ages as a whole. Only recently has this view begun to receive correction. At least the change in outlook has established the variety and contrast which medieval society presents in this as in other fields.

The progress of trade was clearly associated with the rise of the towns to a more prominent position in the economic landscape. The towns had already in the Dark Ages become primarily fortified centres to meet the unsettled conditions of the ages before and after Charlemagne; the connexion is reflected linguistically in such words as the German *burg*, which means both 'castle' and 'town'. The market which satisfied the economic needs of the district was usually situated in the area immediately outside the city walls, a suburban belt known as the *portus*.

As economic connexions became more than purely local, the towns began to take their place as centres of transit and exchange of commodities. Strategic positions on important trade routes helped many towns to increase their economic stature; Venice became the great *entrepôt* for trade with the Middle East, Bruges became the link between the trade of the Baltic and that of the Mediterranean, while for a time in the thirteenth century the fairs of the Champagne towns, situated approximately half-way between the North Sea area and Italy, were the great clearing-house for European trade.

The towns soon began to press for a political and constitutional status more in conformity with their growing economic importance. Relief from the jurisdiction and taxation of feudal hierarchical superiors was the immediate prerequisite and, to achieve this, the townsmen formed themselves into associations bound by oath. The pattern of resemblance to the feudal contract itself is very clear, but there was a striking difference; the compact which led to the autonomy of the towns was one between theoretical equals. The relationship between superior and inferior, the main characteristic of the feudal structure, was absent.

The medieval town structure was no mere revival of the city of classical antiquity, though in countries like Italy there was an obvious continuity of tradition. The main differentiation lay in the fact that, whereas the Graeco-Roman city had been a collection of tribal or familial groups, the medieval town was basically a coming together of individuals bound primarily by an economic nexus. This is not to say that social groupings did not play an important part in medieval urban history; the place of the guilds, shortly to be discussed, would be sufficient refutation. But it is, nevertheless, true that the medieval city was primarily and originally a union of persons rather than of groups or classes, and in this respect it is in marked conformity with the 'personalist' pattern which we have suggested as typical of medieval society as a whole. This truth is particularly applicable in 'The Age of Expansion' of economic growth up to the thirteenth century.

The development of the medieval town is the history of the development of two major institutions – the commune and the guild. These two primary institutions varied in nature and importance from one city or region to another, and often overlapped in function and composition, but broadly speaking it can be said that the commune was essentially a political creation, whereas the guild was economic rather than political.

The area in which the chief growth of autonomous and semi-autonomous urban associations flourished most luxuriantly corresponded roughly with the area of the Carolingian Empire, with England, Spain and the Eastern areas of Germany as subsidiary offshoots. The highest density of population and the most characteristic urban developments occurred in two main centres of commerce, trade and even industrialization – firstly North and Central Italy, secondly Northern France and the Netherlands.

The Italian cities stood, of course, in direct continuity with the Roman classical urban life of the peninsula. No drastic break had occurred; most of the Roman centres had never ceased to exist, despite invasion and depopulation; the number of new centres, such as Venice, was comparatively few. In the immediate post-Carolingian period the towns were officially under the rule of a Count, successor of Charlemagne's local official of that name, and after the establishment of German Imperial rule in Italy from the time of Otto I (middle tenth century) onwards, this agent of Imperial authority was more often than not a bishop. Under them city authority was shared by a small circle of aristocratic

families, the 'patricians'. The nobles in Italy were always more addicted to city life than their northern
counterparts; this is one of the reasons why the feudal
structure was not so firmly rooted south of the Alps.
Country and town were never far apart anywhere in
medieval Europe, but in Italy their interaction was particularly noticeable. It has been suggested that one of
the reasons for the early Italian ascendancy in trade
and commerce was that the pressure of population on
relatively limited agrarian resources could not be solved
as it was in countries like Germany, France and Spain
by expansion and colonization of unexploited territories. 'Commerce,' it has been said, 'was the frontier of
the Italians.'[6]

The conflict between Papacy and Empire in the period
of the Investiture Contest in the eleventh and twelfth
centuries was used by the Italian towns to further their
autonomous status. The bishops of cities such as Milan
were denounced by the Papacy as Imperial nominees
and simoniacs, and in such cities we find the middle and
lower classes of townsmen attacking their secularized
bishops in the name of ecclesiastical reform. The 'commune' made its appearance as the legal description of
the sworn association of citizens which aimed at establishing and preserving the city's newly won autonomy.
The first trace of Italian commune organization was at
Lucca in 1068, but it is clear that the institution must
have been in flourishing existence in Northern and Central Italy previously in the early eleventh century. Its

6. R. S. Lopez, 'Southern Trade', in *The Cambridge Economic
History of Europe*, Vol. II, p. 304. The term 'frontier' is here to be
understood in the technical sense made current by W. P. Webb in
his famous *The Great Frontier* – i.e. a field of expansion into
which an expanding society can penetrate in its search for the
necessary means of economic growth.

growth synchronized with that of Italian commercial expansion overseas. Already in the early eleventh century maritime Italian cities such as Pisa, Genoa, and above all Venice, were snatching control of Mediterranean sea traffic from Islamic powers. The Crusades were largely financed by these wealthy cities and the crusading expansion into the Middle East led to an increased economic turnover for the Crusaders' backers. Trade followed the Cross.

At first the constitutional pattern of the Italian communes was dictated by the power of the upper patrician strata in the cities. Officials known as 'consuls' (an echo of Roman Republican tradition) were elected as heads of State. Originally elections lay in the hands of the whole assembly of citizens but the desire of the patricians to keep a firmer hold on the constitutional process led in most cities to the evolution of a system of indirect election, which lent itself to the retention of governmental power by a self-perpetuating oligarchy. An attempt to avoid the worst consequences of the system by limiting the term of office of the consuls to a single year achieved little but instability and, by the middle of the twelfth century, pressure from the politically unenfranchised lower classes, combined with the threat of reassertion of Imperial authority, forced the city governments to a new expedient. This was the creation of a new governmental organ, the *podesta*, a single official whose powers ran parallel with those of the consuls and were reminiscent of the classical Roman dictator. The *podesta* was entrusted with the particular task of arbitrating between the different factions within the city and was often chosen from outside the city itself as a greater guarantee of his impartiality. In due course, however, this solution was in turn found to have its disadvantages and the demand of lesser merchants and craftsmen for a greater share in urban government now began to exert itself through the pressure of the guilds.

The guilds were the nearest approach in the Middle Ages to the modern Trade Unions and there may indeed be a thread of continuous connexion between them. The origins of the guilds are still greatly debated. Various theories have been put forward about their ancestry. The Roman and Byzantine guilds were certainly economic associations but were strictly controlled by the government and had no autonomous powers of self-government, still less political significance. Some twentieth-century Jewish medievalists have claimed that the Jewish communities were first in the field with guild organization of their own compatriots as early as the tenth century; the so-called *Responsa* literature (recently edited and translated by Professor Agus) certainly reveals a closely knit and legally organized structure which regulates relations among its own members and represents them in their contacts with the outside world. The Jewish organizations, however, were essentially inward-looking and had no ambitions for political control or intervention in a wider context; it is hard, therefore to see them as anticipating the guild structure in all essential respects.

Under a patrician constitution the only way in which the lower middle and artisan classes could make their voices heard was through the formation of an association of originally economic import but which would advance from there in the direction of political influence and even supremacy. It has been pointed out that a parallel development can be observed in medieval Islamic society, when the trade guilds took shape as the vehicles for expression of the underprivileged elements in economic life; to this day the institution is somewhat frowned upon in orthodox Moslem circles.

The classic case of guild supremacy occurred in many Italian cities, where by the thirteenth century the guilds were virtually in political control. In Florence the defeat and humiliation of the nobles by the guildsmen was carried to the extent of making membership of a guild a prerequisite for any right to participate in politics. In Flanders the same process was fought out over the thirteenth and fourteenth centuries and ended in revolt not only against the local feudal overlord, the Count, but even against his suzerain, the King of France.

In the great industrial complexes of Flanders and Tuscany the triumph of the guilds was not the end of economic strife. The issue now became one of struggle between the employers and bankers collected in the 'greater guilds' on the one hand and the artisans of 'the lesser guilds' on the other. The conflict was at its most bitter in the great woollen industry, the most international section of medieval commerce. The Flemish cities had gained their pre-eminence by acting as the manufacturing centre for the raw material provided from England, outstanding for sheep-rearing in the Middle Ages. The two areas were economically interdependent and hence the preservation of a political axis between them was in the interests of both, just as was their mutual opposition to France. The Tuscan cities, particularly Florence, came into the picture as dyers and finishers of the cloth produced in Flanders, but about the turn of the fourteenth century the Italians began to go in for the whole process of cloth-making themselves and the supremacy of Flanders was challenged. It was toppled still further when England, inconvenienced by the Hundred Years War threat to its Flemish markets, embarked on the manufacture of cloth from its own wool. The loss of markets and of raw materials had crippled the Flemish industry by the end of the Middle Ages.

In Italy the venture of clothmaking increased the significance of the more artisan guilds. In Florence a number of proletarian revolts took place during the fourteenth century, though the movement was ultimately crushed.

In France and England the monarchy was able to keep more control of urban organization than elsewhere. Despite the 'commune' movement of the eleventh century, the French towns never succeeded in obtaining the autonomous status prevalent in Flanders, Germany and Italy, while in England the centralizing monarchy kept for itself the monopoly of granting strictly limited urban privileges.

With the fourteenth century a recession set in in both trade and agriculture. An 'Age of Contraction' succeeded to the 'Age of Expansion'. Population again seems to have been the deciding factor. Several factors were responsible for depopulation at this time. The terrible bubonic and pneumonic plague known as the Black Death first appeared in the late 1340s and may have carried off as much as a third of the population. Its ravages were to continue at intervals over the following century. Nor can we overlook the part played by longer, more extensive and more destructive warfare, particularly in France. A less dramatic reason for the demographic recession may have been that further opportunities for exploitation of uncultivated or undercultivated land had now dried up. The German drive across the Elbe which had commenced in the tenth century and had extended German territory to its present-day limits at the expense of the Slavs was at an end; so was the large-scale reclamation of swamp, coastland and forest which had been such an impressive feature of the earlier period.

Depopulation affected both trade and agriculture. For the peasants it was to some extent an advantage. There was now more land per head to go round and the shortage of labour put the peasants in a stronger bargaining position. Conservative legislation such as the Statute and Ordinance of Labourers in England could not arrest the trend. Individualism was replacing the feudal contractual relationship as the motivating force for both lords and peasantry. In the case of the peasants the old *manse* unit, in which several generations might be living side by side, gave place more and more to the cellular one-family unit which has become the basis of domestic life in the West in modern times. The nobility in their turn reacted to the new conditions by aiming at a more intensive exploitation of their lands at the expense of tenant and common rights. The latter, being often unwritten, could the more easily be set aside with a greater emphasis on statute law. The 'enclosure' movement, which appropriated for the landlords common arable land which was then transformed into sheep-runs for the benefit of the woollen industry, was a leading manifestation of the way things were going. For landlord and peasant alike private profit became the acknowledged order of the day.

In the towns the age of contraction favoured a reverse process. The shrinking of markets and the heavy competition for what remained led to the end of the old adventurous free-for-all atmosphere of earlier days, in which men like Godric had made fortunes. The guilds now began to take control of the situation with a protectionistic outlook and increasingly rigid organization. Attempts at economic 'autarky' favoured the increasing protectionism; the application of tariff barriers and even the complete prohibition of certain imports might sometimes seem to be the best way to encourage native industries in an infant stage. The growing intervention of the centralizing monarchies in France, England and Spain was also exercised in the same direction.

The age of contraction had sharpened the social conflicts within the towns. The fourteenth century saw risings of the urban lower classes all over Western Europe from England to Bohemia. The usual fate of these risings was repression, but in most cases the urban upper classes could only ride the storm by handing over political control to a dictator, unofficial or official, or by coming to terms with the reinvigorated monarchies. The great age of urban autonomy was over by the time the Middle Ages themselves drew to a close.

The cultural products of the medieval city are fascinatingly diverse. In literature the vernacular came of age and its resources were exploited to the full by writers such as Dante in Italy, Ruteboeuf and Villon in France, Chaucer in England. The bourgeois class became literate originally for commercial purposes; banking and accounting were their inventions and literacy was essential for the operation of these new facilities. Naturally they did not halt at ledgers and account books; once the new art was acquired, the lay demand for more varied reading matter was inevitable. In the fourteenth and fifteenth centuries books of both a secular and religious nature multiplied among the growing lay reading public. The arrival of the printing press was the only ultimate method of matching supply to demand.

It is hard to see how the universities could have come into being in any other *milieu* than that of the towns. Their parent seems to have been the cathedral school, that relic of Charlemagne's educational reforms. To these establishments in the eleventh and twelfth centuries came freelance teachers and freelance students, absorbed with a passion for exploring knowledge through the medium of the revived science of dialectic, which was now replacing rhetoric as the foundation of education.

At first a system of private initiative prevailed. Teachers dispensed instruction in return for fees; students transferred from one master to another at will, bitter competition for pupils often taking place. The so-called 'Goliardic' school of poetry reveals the existence of a clerical proletariat, most of it in no more than minor orders, who wandered about as intellectual beggars, using their learning to attack spiritual and temporal establishments. One wonders if their nickname points to a peasant origin for many of these dissident clerics; for the nobility Goliath was the symbol of the uncouth peasantry.

Eventually the situation crystallized in the direction of function and specialization. The universities took shape as corporate institutional bodies, provided by royal and papal charters, and separated into faculties according to the subject of teaching. Except in centres specializing in law (like Bologna) or medicine (like Padua or Salerno) they were clerical in composition (like Paris or Oxford), with Arts (still based on the Seven Liberal Arts) leading up to theology as the basis of their studies. Teachers banded together into organizations somewhat parallel to the economic guilds, holding a monopoly of teaching rights for their members; by the beginning of the thirteenth century the old freelance days were over. Entrance into the ranks of the masters was regulated by a series of examinations leading to the conferring of 'degrees'. Instruction followed the pattern of reading and explaining standard authorities in a word-by-word fashion ('lectures'), while examinations were conducted in the form of the 'disputation', a verbal encounter in which an opinion was attacked and defended according to rules of dialectical argument. A work such as St Thomas Aquinas' *Summa Theologiae* (*c.* 1270) shows how the highest flights of philosophy and theology could be engaged in while still conforming faithfully to the dialectical technique.

Up to the eleventh century philosophy and theology (and there was little distinction between the two) were dominated by St Augustine's version of Platonism. Both were essentially regarded as dialogues between the soul and God, dialogues which depended at every stage on Divine illumination; such illumination could be granted either directly or indirectly through the medium of bona fide authority. The mystical contact between the believer and God under the benign guidance of authority was the natural *milieu* of Christian speculation in the pre-Scholastic period; primarily designed for the monastic communities and best followed within their framework, this phase of Christian thought was intensely Biblical and patristic, though it was prepared to make almost indiscriminate use of non-Christian symbolism. The result was often a confusion of unrelated, unorganized analogies, held together by the circumscribing boundary of the Faith without much regard for the rationality of the consequent conglomerate. One is reminded of the strange combination of solid simplicity with fantastic proliferation of gratuitous, almost unrelated detail which characterized the Romanesque ecclesiastical architecture of the same period.

This disregard of the pre-Scholastic period for the strict pursuit of rational arguments is further shown by its toleration of striking discrepancies among its own recognized authorities. An Augustinian caveat on the presumption of too much reliance on individual reason prevented the too free cross-questioning of authorities.

A decisive social change in the intellectual milieu came with the association of the universities with the more fluid and richly changing life of the towns. The universities, following the pattern of the towns in which they were situated, became centres of production, exchange and competition – but of ideas rather than material commodities. The typical intellectual dialogue was now no longer solely a dialogue of the soul with God under the aegis of authority. It now became also a dialogue of one thinker with another, thrashing out debatable points in the light of rational argument. The necessity to argue led to a crystallization and clarification of methods of thinking.

We can see the new mood exemplified in Abélard's famous *Sic et Non* ('Yes and No') composition. Here Abélard collected and juxtaposed differing authorities on theological themes without attempting to harmonize them. In the field of Canon Law at about the same time (*c.* 1140) Gratian made a more positive application of the same method. In his *Concordance of Discordant Canons* (to be known usually as the *Decretum*) Gratian tried to iron out discrepancies and did so convincing a job that his compilation became the nucleus of the official Western code of Canon Law.

The greater prominence of the element of struggle between individual viewpoints which the new dialectical technique emphasized found its counterpart in the actual subject matter of philosophical discussion. The problem of 'universals' is the obvious example. The older 'Realist' school thought of the world as dependent on certain archetypal ideal patterns which alone were real and alone gave significance to individual phenomena. To this was now opposed the so-called

'Nominalist' theory, which asserted that the individual alone possessed reality, the ideal archetypes being merely convenient names to describe groups of similar individual persons or objects. Abélard attempted to mediate between the rival camps by a 'moderate realist' position which argued that valid universal qualities could be perceived by the mind in individual objects by a process of abstraction or perception of a common relationship. Thus Abélard argues that there is no universal species of Man existing over and above the individuals forming the species; but there is a common human status which is inherent in and shared by all these individuals. Medieval philosophy had become and was to remain an explanation of relationships.

A system which sets out to investigate the universe in terms of relational interactions needs a complete and elaborate methodology of definition and clarification. The characteristic Scholastic technique and terminology, which reached its apogee in the thirteenth century, provided such a methodology. The elaborate subdivisions and almost irritatingly minute carefulness of the Scholastic vocabulary were intended to convey all the elements necessary to solve the given problem under discussion, together with a clear indication of their resemblances and differences. It has been pointed out that our own modern system of scholarly reference and citation of books is derived from the medieval Scholastics.

The *Summa Theologiae* of St Thomas Aquinas is the classic achievement of the Scholastic method. Aquinas' motivation is expressed in his own dictum, 'Grace does not destroy Nature but it fulfils it,' and this standpoint enabled him to give both Reason and Faith their respective dues. In his proofs of the existence of God Aquinas refused to make use of any but rational arguments. His theory of knowledge replaced the Augustinian 'illumination' theory by an epistemology based on sense perception. He used the concept of Natural Law to emphasize the participation of Man by reason in the Divine ordering of the universe.

In the fourteenth century the Scholastic system was used to more destructive effect. William of Ockham argued that only empirically observable facts could be regarded as demonstrable by reason; all else must be regarded as falling within the sphere of Faith. Ockham was a fideist rather than a sceptic; he was no medieval Hume but was concerned, as he imagined, with clarifying in a more satisfactory way than his predecessors the boundary between objects of knowledge ascertainable by reason and those which could only be known by non-rational means. This aim led him to throw over the compromise solution to the problem of universals put forward by Abélard and refined by Aquinas and to deny that metaphysics could take ultimate account of anything but the individual. The mind may form a concept of a universal species but this concept is dependent on an observed similarity between individuals and on that alone.

The Ockhamist school became the *nouvelle vague* and stormy petrel of later medieval philosophy. Its denial of rational cogency to all but strictly empirical proof led some of its adherents to the very borders of scepticism. Nicholas of Autrecourt denied the principle of causation and maintained that objects of knowledge were ultimately determinable by the mind.

A more objective and optimistic investigation of the outer world by empirical rational observation was made by certain Parisian Ockhamists, working in the realm of the natural sciences, particularly physics. The traditional picture of the universe was as much ethical as physical; deriving largely from Aristotle and Ptolemy, it envisaged the universal order as being governed by qualitative and purposive relationship between its parts. The Ockhamist scepticism about the possibility of proof of this teleological cosmic relationship led to a concentration on investigation of individual phenomena and the consequent vindication for natural science of its own autonomous field.

Gothic architecture, like Scholasticism, was a town product. Both movements in fact originated from the same area of Northern France which had also been the cradle of classic feudalism. A number of modern writers, particularly Erwin Panofsky, have traced a remarkable series of parallels between the Gothic and Scholastic techniques. The careful articulation and clarification characteristic of Scholastic methodology is paralleled by the organization of 'units in unity' (if we may coin a phrase) which is the essential feature of the thirteenth-century High Gothic cathedral. The individualism of Ockham and his followers may be paralleled, as Panofsky argues, by the gradual dissolution of Gothic unity into the fantastic elaboration of the Decorated and Flamboyant styles. The same trend may be observed in painting, particularly in the increasing desire to portray the individual, 'warts and all' (one thinks of Van Eyck's Canon Van der Paele), and even more in the invention of perspective, which equated realism with the standpoint of the individual observer.

Both Scholasticism and Gothic were in fact expressions of an urban Catholic Christianity, just as the monastic mystical tradition of philosophy and the Romanesque tradition of architecture had been expressions of a feudal Catholic Christianity.

Finally, we must not forget the part played by the medieval towns in the development of technology. The divorce between pure science and technology in the Middle Ages has often been pointed out. The former remained somewhat sterile until the fourteenth century. One reason for this was the tendency to subordinate detailed investigation of phenomena to the construction of an overall model of the universe; the systematization of metaphysical reasoning, particularly after the rediscovery of Aristotle in the twelfth and thirteenth centuries, left little room (except among some of the Ockhamists) for scientific inquiry in the modern sense. Another factor was the medieval respect for 'authorities' – Ptolemy in astronomy, Galen in medicine, Aristotle in physics, were assumed to have provided the ultimate truth in each of their fields and this discouraged further original inquiry. It is also true that the border between rational science and magic was not very closely drawn; even those best equipped to achieve advance in scientific investigation were apt to be sidetracked by the quest for the philosopher's stone.

In the purely technological field no such inhibiting factors were present. Here everyday needs were paramount and their satisfaction could be attempted without reference to academic speculation. The windmill, the mechanical clock (needed by the growing busy merchant class for which time was literally becoming money), spectacles, gunpowder and the mechanical crank all emerge in the period between 1150 and 1450. The characteristic Western ideal of manipulating the forces of nature for the benefit of human needs and comforts seems here to be already present.

6

EPILOGUE: MEDIEVAL GOVERNMENT
AND ITS DILEMMA

THE medieval social structure had involved the Christian
Church intimately with the temporal establishment. But
on what terms?

In the late fifth century Pope Gelasius I had tried to
provide a working formula to explain the relationship
between the spiritual and secular powers. He had argued
that each authority had its own sphere of action, allotted
to it by God, that neither ought to interfere in the work
of the other, but that in the last resort the spiritual
power should have the supreme voice, because it was
concerned with the salvation of the souls of all the
community, including that of the secular ruler himself.
Gelasius' dualism is not drafted with anything other
than a Christian society in mind.

Though often quoted in the Middle Ages, Gelasius'
solution proved impossible to implement. His remarks
had not clarified the vexed question of the delimitation
of the border line between the two authorities, and, in
any case, the current of the early Middle Ages was running strongly against even such precision as he was
able to achieve. As we have seen, the tendency of the
period before the twelfth century was to conflate and
confuse the spheres of reason and faith, of spiritual and
secular affairs, of personality and institution, and the
concept of government did not escape the general process of blurring.

The usual medieval secular governmental structure was

based on the institution of Kingship. The King is represented in the coronation rituals as dedicated by his office to the preservation of the laws of the community, the rights and privileges of all his subjects under the law and the protection of the Church. The anointing ritual, the focal point of the whole ceremony, was a semi-religious act administered by the chief ecclesiastic of the realm and was thought to confer on the King the direct support of God. In the early Middle Ages anointing was popularly supposed to have a quasi-sacramental character and to invest the King with virtually priestly powers. In some quarters the anointed King was even thought to have acquired miraculous faculties of healing the sick.

The sacrosanct character which Christianity conferred on the King reached its highest theoretical extension with the creation of a Christian Western Roman Empire under Charlemagne and his successors. Although Imperial authority was eventually confined in practice to Germany, an aura of past and potential universality hung about the office. The Emperor, crowned by the Pope and invested with majestic though vague authority over the Christian community as a whole, could easily assume the mantle of Constantine and his Caesaro-Papist successors. The comparative powerlessness of the Church in the centuries after Charlemagne assisted the trend.

At the same time there were ecclesiastical attempts to maintain independence by insisting on the right of the episcopate to advise, warn and if necessary depose a Christian King. Louis the Pious, Charlemagne's own son, after a clash with the Frankish episcopate, was forced to make a humiliating submission and this insistence on the full implications of the Gelasian theory was taken up by the Papacy during the Investiture

Contest between Pope Gregory VII and Emperor Henry IV. This conflict arose over the issue of the control of appointments to high ecclesiastical offices, but became a general struggle for supreme authority over the Church. The Papacy's venerable claims, established in early Christian centuries but obscured by infiltration of the secular authority, had been reasserted by the so-called Election Decree of 1059, which reserved the choice of Pope to the College of Cardinals, his immediate entourage, and expressly ruled out any secular participation in the election. The fight between the two authorities was waged on the common ground of acceptance of the premise of a single Christian society with both spiritual and political aspects. This conflation prevented the re-emergence of a conception of impersonal public authority such as the classical Roman State had known. The decentralization of authority represented by feudalism and its personal relationship was another weakening link in the formulation of a political outlook based on the sense of a corporate community. The response of royal authority to the feudal challenge varied from country to country. We have already noticed that in France and England, strongly feudalized countries, the feudal relationship could actually be used for an eventual strengthening of royal authority. The 'conventional' notion of many Christian thinkers about human government as part remedy, part punishment for the Fall of Man, led to a depreciatory view of political institutions and activity.

The position began to change round about the time of the economic, social and cultural revivals of the tenth and subsequent centuries. With the loss of distrust for human reason and its achievements came a gradual strengthening of belief in the natural character of political life as beneficial for man and corresponding to an inherent need of his being. Classical sources familiar to the medieval philosophers of the twelfth century, particularly Cicero and the *Timaeus* dialogue by Plato, had spoken of Nature as the inspiration of the life of men in society. But the biggest single source of the revival of belief in the naturalness of political activity was the return of knowledge of Roman Law as collected by Justinian in his *Corpus of Civil Law*. This was beginning to be studied in the Italian legal schools, particularly Bologna, in the eleventh century. Throughout the Middle Ages Bologna was to remain the great centre of legal studies for both Civil and Canon Law.

The 'two Laws' did in fact move very much on parallel lines. The legal organization of the Church centred on the monarchical government of the Papacy, just as the rising national monarchies and city states utilized Roman Civil Law to sharpen their own growing sense of corporate solidarity and public government. In both cases much use was made of the principle of representation, though in a somewhat different sense from the meaning attached to it today.

Roman classical practice had confined representation to the sphere of private law. In a lawsuit one of the parties might delegate the conduct of his case and complete responsibility for accepting or making a settlement to a proctor or legal expert. In the Middle Ages the principle was applied to public law to form the basis of the first representative assemblies. These assemblies were composed of persons chosen by the influential sections of the community to counsel the King, listen to his requests, consent to them and devise means of complying with them. The possibility of lack of consent to monarchical wishes was regarded as undesirable and unthinkable, though in practice it sometimes happened. Thus medieval representative assemblies submitted to an amount of royal manipulation and control which would clearly be resented by their modern descendants.

The difference lies in the much broader interpretation given to the notion of representation by medieval political thought. The idea of an assembly standing for the estates and interests of the Kingdom was only one aspect of the medieval conception. A much larger place was occupied by the political significance of the monarch himself, who thanks to Roman Law became a public as well as a personal symbol. By the end of the Middle Ages the Tudor lawyer Edmund Plowden was able to talk of the King in England as possessing 'two bodies', one 'natural' and one 'politic', the latter being 'a Body that cannot be seen or handled, consisting of Policy and Government, and constituted for the Direction of the People and the Management of the public weal.'

This 'body politic' was linked with the conception, elaborated from Roman Law's presentation of Imperial prerogatives, of the *status* of the monarch. The conception of *status* expressed the idea that the monarch represented in his person and office the full public authority of the community. Thus the *status* of the Church was articulated in the authority of the Pope and that of the secular community in that of the King. In theories about the King a considerable number of feudal 'personalist' ideas survived and were attached particularly to the King's private possessions, which were none too closely differentiated from his public obligations and prerogatives. The legal distinction between the *status regis* ('*status* of the King) and the *status regni* ('*status* of the Kingdom') was a move towards a differentiation.

It is clear that the origin of representative assemblies is to be found in the extension of the notion of 'the body politic' of the monarch. The dignity and authority of the monarchy could be emphasized, even enhanced, if the King associated with his governmental activity a cross-section of his more important subjects. Henry VIII was to put the matter succinctly: 'We be informed by our judges that we at no time stand so highly in our estate royal as in the time of parliament, wherein we as head and you as members are conjoined and knit together in one body politic.' Similarly medieval canonists envisaged the Papal monarchy as enjoying an increase of dignity when surrounded by the deliberations of the episcopate in a General Council.

The representative principle was more difficult to apply to the Church than to the secular political community. The Papacy claimed that its monarchical authority rested on a direct grant from God through the Divine promises made to St Peter, and it was thus obvious that undiluted application of the principle of representation could not be made as far as the Church as a whole was concerned. The thirteenth century saw, however, a remarkable list of applications of the principle to subsidiary bodies within the Church. The Dominican Order of friars adopted representation as its constitutional principle from its foundation in the early thirteenth century, while a whole series of cathedral chapters and guilds did likewise, and bodies such as the English Convocation, elected on representative lines, paralleled the line of development of the secular parliaments. There were even tentative moves to emphasize the position of the College of Cardinals as a type of permanent representative council round the Pope.

The Great Schism in the Papacy at the end of the fourteenth and beginning of the fifteenth centuries showed the explosive possibilities of representation when applied to Church government. The dispute between rival claimants to the Papal office (at one stage no less than three were disputing the allegiance of Christendom) led to the desperate assertion by some thinkers that a General Council representing the faithful had the right and duty to settle the Schism and reimpose unity in the Church. The exponents of the 'Conciliar theory' argued that the General Council was intrinsically superior to the Papacy in the Government of the Church. The Papacy was triumphant but the unsettlement and questioning of the Conciliar period prepared the ground for the Reformation.

Secular governments, too, eventually found difficulties with their representative assemblies. Only in England did the cooperation between monarch and parliament achieve fruition and even there, as seventeenth-century events were to show, the issue of ultimate supremacy was inescapable. Elsewhere in Western Europe the upsurge of monarchical strength during the early modern period went side by side with the premature atrophy of representative assemblies.

The dilution of Christianity by the world into which it came is a permanent hazard of the Gospel. The tragedy of the Middle Ages was that often the very methods adopted with the intention of facing the hazard successfully ended by falling victim to it. The agents of reform in one century could well be its opponents in a later age. The Benedictines, founded as an escape from the spirit of the world in the sixth century, had become large landed proprietors by the eighth. The most magnificent of all reforming attempts, that of St Francis of Assisi in the thirteenth century, tried to solve the problem by forbidding property ownership to the Franciscans altogether, individually or collectively, the prohibition of collective ownership being a formidable innovation. But comfort and learning exercised their fascinations and within a century the ardent idealism of the founder had been swamped in an elaborate dispute between the Papacy and the Order on the legal nature of property and poverty.

The development of the Franciscan dispute takes us perhaps to the heart of the failure of medieval Christian society. Based, as we have previously seen, on the concept of a 'personalist' relation between God and Man, Man and his neighbour, medieval Christendom had striven to protect this ideal by institutionalizing it. The relation of the believer to God was to be protected by the formulations and institutions of the Church, the relations of men with each other by institutions such as feudalism, the urban corporations and guilds, the universities, and, above all, the political public authority. By the fifteenth century disenchantment with all these institutional forms was being expressed on a large scale. The corruption and over-centralization of the Church bureaucracy, the failure of the landlord-tenant relationship to keep pace with changing agrarian conditions, the fossilization of the guilds and universities into self-perpetuating oligarchies, were all so many examples of the betrayal of medieval ideals by the very institutions designed to protect them. With the Renaissance and the Reformation, indeed the Counter-Reformation, the movements of discontent and protest become open. A search for new institutions, new formulations of personal and social relationships, even new worlds, begins. All over Western Europe, though with varying pace and in varying forms, medieval is passing into modern.

Looking back over the centuries to the comparatively tiny medieval Christian West from a Europe which has become the world, one does not need to elaborate on differences. It is perhaps more to the point to realize that the fundamental problem which the Middle Ages failed to solve is still with us. We are still faced with the same necessity to implement ideals of human relationship through socially viable institutions, but how to strike a just balance between individual and institution is as doubtfully debated as ever it was. The issues of modern civilization are more grandiose, if not more complex, than those of its medieval parent, and yet it has much to learn from its ancestor. History is not always at its best when it is utilitarian, but a sympathetic knowledge of the problems of our own past may allow us, not only to use hindsight to give clearer solutions to those problems than the men of the past themselves could provide, but even to take calmer stock of the difficulties and opportunities of the present.

SELECT BIBLIOGRAPHY

THIS list makes no pretence whatever to be exhaustive. The author has merely attempted to indicate works which he has found useful and which may also be useful to his readers. As a general rule the list has been confined to works available in English but other works have been occasionally included where no comparable work appears to be available in English. The place of publication of all works mentioned is London, unless otherwise stated.

GENERAL WORKS

The relevant volumes in the *Methuen History of Europe* series (by M. Deanesley, Z. N. Brooke, C. W. Prévité-Orton and W. T. Waugh respectively) still remain the best overall survey in English. For reference purposes they should be supplemented by *The Cambridge Medieval History* (now in process of revision). The sections of maps attached to each volume are the best available.

For all major aspects of the medieval scene, *The Legacy of the Middle Ages* (edited by G. C. Crump and E. F. Jacob, 1926), is still worth consulting.

Moss, H. St L. B., *The Birth of the Middle Ages, 395–814*, 1935.
Southern, R. W., *The Making of the Middle Ages*, 1953.
Heer, F., *The Medieval World: Europe, 1100–1350*, 1961.
Huizinga, J., *The Waning of the Middle Ages*, 1924.
    Culture and society in the fourteenth and fifteenth centuries.
Talbot-Rice, D. (Ed.), *The Dark Ages*, 1965.
Evans, J. (Ed.), *The Flowering of the Middle Ages*, 1966.
    Both these collective works are magnificently illustrated.
Le Goff, J., *La civilisation de l'occident médiéval*, Paris, 1965.
    An impressive one-man synthesis. The many apt illustrations
    are a feature.
Drew, R. F. and Lear, F. S. (Eds.) *Perspectives in Medieval History*,
    New York, 1964.

A bird's-eye view of changing interpretations of medieval history by modern scholarship.

ANTHOLOGIES

Coulton, G. G., *Life in the Middle Ages* (one volume edition), 1935. A collection of translated sources on many topics.

Ross, J. B. and McLaughlin, M. M., *The Portable Medieval Reader*, New York, 1949.

Flores, A., *Medieval Age*, 1965.
Various modern translations of poetry between the ninth and fifteenth centuries.

CHAPTER 2

Rostovtzeff, M., *Social and Economic History of the Roman Empire*, 1926.

The Cambridge Economic History of Europe, Vol. I ('The Agrarian Life of the Middle Ages'), revised edition, 1966.

Mazzarino, S., *The End of the Ancient World*, 1966.
A remarkable survey of changing views of the reasons for the fall of Rome. The survey deals with views from the third century to the present.

Boissonnade, P., *Life and Work in Medieval Europe*, 1927.

Dopsch, A., *Economic and Social Foundations of European Civilization*, 1937.

Pirenne, H., *Mohammed and Charlemagne*, 1939.

Latouche, R., *The Birth of Western Economy*, 1961.

Bark, W. C., *Origins of the Medieval World*, 1958.

Gagé, J., *Les classes sociales dans l'empire romain*, Paris, 1964.

Jones, A. H. M., *The Later Roman Empire*, 3 vols., 1964.

Jones, A. H. M., *The Decline of the Ancient World*, 1966.

Cohn, N., *The Pursuit of the Millennium*, 1957.

Runciman, S., *A History of the Crusades*, 3 vols., 1951–4.

Almgren, B. (Ed.), *The Viking*, 1966.

CHAPTER 3

Deanesley, M., *A History of the Medieval Church, 590–1500*, 1925.

Gough, M., *The Early Christians*, 1961.

Bolgar, R. R., *The Classical Heritage and its Beneficiaries*, 1954.
The best detailed survey of the impact of Graeco-Roman literature on the Middle Ages.

Laistner M. L. W., *Thought and Letters in Western Europe, A.D. 500–900*, revised edition, 1957.

Gilson, E., *The Christian Philosophy of St Augustine*, 1960.

Cochrane, C. N. S., *Christianity and Classical Culture*, 1940.

Leclerq, H., *The Love of Learning and the Desire for God*, 1961.
A study of the monastic culture of the pre-Scholastic period.

CHAPTER 4

Thompson, E. A., *The Visigoths in the Time of Ulfila*, 1966.

Bloch, M., *Feudal Society*, 1961.
The standard work.

Bloch, M., *French Rural Society*, 1966.

Valency, M., *In Praise of Love*, 1958.
An account of the development of the courtly love tradition.

Lewis, C. S., *The Allegory of Love*, 1936.

Dawson, C., 'The Origins of Romanticism' in *Medieval Essays*, 1953.
Argues for the Arabic origin of the courtly love ethic.

Gilson, E., *Héloïse and Abélard*, 1951.

Sherwin Bailey, D., *The Man-Woman Relationship in Christian Thought*, 1959.

Lynn White, Jr., *Medieval Technology and Social Change*, 1962.

Oursel, R., *Les pélerins du moyen âge: les hommes, les chemins, les sanctuaires*, Paris, 1963.
An account of every aspect of medieval pilgrimages.

Lamb, H. H., *The Changing Climate*, 1966.
Contains some valuable articles on the history of medieval weather.

Knowles, D., *From Pachomius to Ignatius*, 1966.
The constitutional history of the medieval religious orders.

CHAPTER 5

The Cambridge Economic History of Europe, Vol. II ('Trade and Industry in the Middle Ages'), 1952, and Vol. III ('Economic Organization and Policies in the Middle Ages'), 1963.

Pirenne, H., *Medieval Cities*, New York, 1925.

Weber, M., *The City*, 1958.

Agus, I. A., *Urban Civilization in Pre-Crusade Europe*, 2 vols., Leiden, 1965.

Le Goff, J., *Les intellectuels du moyen âge*, Paris, 1957.

Rashdall, H., *The Medieval Universities* (revised edition by Powicke, F. M. and Emden, A. B.), 1936.

Weinberg, J. R., *A Short History of Medieval Philosophy*, Princeton, 1964.

Gilson, E., *Christian Philosophy in the Middle Ages*, 1955.

Lewis, C. S., *The Discarded Image*, 1964.
  A clear account of the various elements in the make-up of the medieval world picture.

Frankl, P., *Gothic Architecture*, 1962.

Frankl, P., *The Gothic: Literary Sources and Interpretations through Eight Centuries*, 1960.

Panofsky, E., *Gothic Architecture and Scholasticism*, 1951.

CHAPTER 6

McIlwain, C. H., *The Growth of Political Thought in the West*, New York, 1932.

Morrall, J. B., *Political Thought in Medieval Times*, 2nd ed., 1960.

Ehler, S. Z. and Morrall, J. B., *Church and State through the Centuries*, 1954.

Kern, F., *Kingship and Law in the Middle Ages*, 1939.

Kantorowicz, E., *The King's Two Bodies*, Princeton, 1957.

Post, G., *Studies in Medieval Legal Thought*, Princeton, 1964.

Ullmann, W. A., *A History of Political Thought: The Middle Ages*, 1965.

D'Entrèves, A. P., *The Medieval Contribution to Political Thought*, 1939.

Tierney, B., *Foundations of the Conciliar Theory*, 1955.

INDEX

Abélard, 118, 119, 151, 152

Agobard of Lyons, 84

Agus, I. A. 144

Alcuin, 88, 93

Alexander the Great, 33, 55

Alexis, St, Life of, 111

Alfred the Great, 47, 78

Al Hakim I, 108, 121

Altabiskar, Song of, 111

Annales Ecclesiastici (*Baronius*) 17

Anselm, St, 109

Antonio, 137

Aristotle, 74, 76, 153, 155

Arthur, King, 44

Atawulf, 43

Aucassin, 39–40

Aucassin and Nicolette, 39–40

Augustine of Canterbury, St, 44

Augustine of Hippo, St, 12, 13, 38, 53, 57–72, 74, 76, 77, 89, 91, 94, 95, 117, 150

Augustus, 33, 35

Autolycus, 137

Bacon F. 20, 118

Bark, W. C., 28

Baronius, 17

Battle of the Books (Swift), 20

Bayeux Tapestry, 113

Beatrice, 124

Beatriz de Dia, 122

Beaufort, Margaret, 128

Benedict, St, 102

Benedict, St, Rule of, 87, 115

Benedict of Aniane, 87, 115

Bernard of Clairvaux, St, 109, 129

Bernard of Ventadour, 122

Bertram de Born, 129

Bloch, M, 133

Boccaccio, 127

Boethius, 74–8, 91

Boniface, St, 83

Bossuet, 12, 13, 17

Burckhardt, J., 8, 25

Capellanus, Andreas, 41

Capitularies (*Charlemagne*), 96

Caracalla, 34

Cassiodorus, 91

Cellarius, 13, 14

Centuries of Magdeburg (Flacius Illyricus), 16

Cercamon, 123

Chansons, 77, 111, 112, 119

Charlemagne, 17, 31, 42, 47, 50, 82–8, 96, 97, 109, 111, 133, 148, 157

Charles Martel, 83, 85, 88

Chateaubriand, 24

Chaucer, 78, 127, 148

Chesterton, 24

Christine de Pisan, 127

Cicero, 70, 90, 159

City of God (St Augustine of Hippo), 60, 62–72, 84

Civilisation of the Renaissance in Italy (Burckhardt), 25

Clement of Alexandria, 57

Clovis, 47, 80

Cobbett, 24

Cohn, N., 42

Coke, E., 19

Commodian, 60, 72

Communist Manifesto (Marx and Engels), 26

Confessions (St Augustine of Hippo), 62

Constantine the Great, 14, 30, 31, 32, 50, 52, 55, 65, 82, 99, 157

Constantine, Donation of, 82

Convivio (Dante), 77

Corpus of Civil Law (Justinian), 159

Coulborn, R., 22

Coulton, 24

Cromwell, O., 19

Cujas, 20

Dante, 49, 124, 127, 148

Decameron (Boccaccio), 127

De Consolatione Philosophiae (Boethius), 76–8

Decretum (Gratian), 151

De Doctrina Christiana (St Augustine of Hippo), 58

De Fide Catholica (Boethius), 76

De Musica (St Augustine of Hippo), 59

Dietrich of Bern (Theodoric), 79

Diocletian, 31, 32–3, 37, 99

Dionysius the Areopagite, 93 94–5

Divine Comedy (Dante), 124

Dopsch, A., 46

Dream of the Road, 108

Dream of Scipio, 90

Dubois, P., 50

Eleanor of Aquitaine, 122

Eriugena, John Scotus, 92–7

Essay on Criticism (Pope), 18, Eve, 117

Feudalism in History (Coulborn), 22

Flacius Illyricus, 16

Flamenca, 124

Francis of Assisi, St, 162

Frederick Barbarossa, 42

Freeman, J. R., 24

Galen, 155

Ganelon, 113

Gelasius I, 156

Geoffrey of Monmouth, 44

Germania (Tacitus), 100

Gibbon, 18, 28, 38, 56

Gilson, E., 93

Godfrey de Bouillon, 112

Godric, St, 137–8

Goliath, 115, 129, 149

Golden Legend, 129

Gottfried of Strasbourg, 124, 127

Gottschalk, 91, 93

Gratian, 151

Greene, G., 94

Gregory the Great, St, 16, 58, 59, 82

Gregory VII, St,, 113, 158

Gregory of Tours, 80

Guillaume de Lorris, 126–7

Hadrian, 74

Harold, King, 24

Harrington, 19

Hegel, 12, 13, 22, 38
Héloise, 118, 119
Henry II, King of England, 122
Henry IV, Emperor, 113, 158
Henry VIII, King of England, 161
Heraclitus, 11
Hippolytus, 72
History of Reformation (Cobbett), 24
Hetman, 19
Hugo, V., 24
Hume, D., 153
Huss, 16

Ibn Hazm, 121
Ibn Saud, 45
Irminon, 102
Irminon, Polptyque of, 102
Isabella of Bavaria, 128
Isidore, St, 79

Jean de Mun, 126, 127
Jerome, St, 57, 60, 76, 118
Jesu, dulcis memoria (St Bernard), 110
Joachites, 16
John of Salisbury, 40
Jones, A. H. M., 37
Justinian the Great, 43, 79, 159

Knowles, D., 115
Kropotkin, 25–6

La Popelinière, 20
Langland, 40
Lanternari, V., 42
Latouche, R., 46
Lenin, 38
Leo III, Pope, 84
Leo X, Pope, 25
Levellers, 19, 24

Lex Romana Visigothorum, 73
Lives of the Artists (Vasari), 15
Louis the Pious, 157
Lovejoy, A. O., 93
Luke, St, Gospel of, 69
Lull, Ramon, 50
Luther, 16
Lynn White, Jr, 131

Mabillon, 20
Macrobius, 90
Magna Carta, 19
Maistre, J. de, 23
Malory, 44
Margaret of Anjou, 128
Mark, King of Cornwall, 122, 125
Martianus Capella, 91
Martin, A. von, 27
Marx, K., 26–7, 63
Maximian, 35
Maximus the Confessor, 93
Memorare (St Bernard), 129
Mercury and Philology, Marriage of (Martianus Capella), 91
Meroveus, 81
Michelet, 22
Miller's Tale (Chaucer), 127
Milton, 17
Mohammed, 45, 49
Mohammed and Charlemagne (Pirenne), 46
More, St Thomas, 128
Muratori, 20

Napoleon I, 86
Natural History (Pliny the Elder), 133
New Christianity (Saint-Simon), 25

New Science (Vico), 21
Nicholas of Autrecourt, 153
Nicolette, 39
Nibelungenlied, 109

O'Casey, S., 11
Oceana (Harrington), 19
Ockham, William of, 153–4
Olaf Tryggvason, 47
Origen, 57
Otto the Great, 50
Ovid, 90

Palmieri, 14, 15
Panofsky, E., 159
Passion of St Saba, 101
Paul, St, 55, 60, 93, 117
Pepin, 81–2
Peter, St, 161
Peter the Venerable, 48
Phenomenology of Mind
   (Hegel), 22
Philo, 89
Piers Plowman (Langland), 40
Plato, 74, 76, 90, 124, 128, 159
Pliny the Elder, 133
Pliny the Younger, 100
Plowden, E., 160
Policraticus (John of Salisbury),
   40
Pope, A., 18
Post, G., 28
Postan, M. N., 139
Procopius, 44
Ptolemy, 153–5
Pursuit of the Millennium
   (Cohn), 42

Rabanus Maurus, 92
Ranke, L. von, 23
Reeve's Tale (Chaucer), 127
Reginald of Durham, 137–8

Religions of the Oppressed
   (Lanternari), 42
Republic (Cicero), 70, 90
Responsa literature, 144
Roland, 48, 109, 112, 113, 114
Roland, Song of, 34, 111–14
Romance of the Rose, 126–7
Rostovtzeff, M., 35
Ruteboeuf, 149

Saint-Simon, 25
Salvian, 37
Sanori, A., 28
Sarrazin, 95
Scott, W., 24
Septimus Severus, 34
Sic et Non (Abélard), 151
Simon, R., 20
Sociology of the Renaissance
   (von Martin), 27
Sordello, 123, 127
Spelman, H., 19
Stephen, St, King of Hungary,
   50
Stephen, King of England, 120
Stephen III, Pope, 82
Stuarts, 19
Stubbs, 24
Summa Theologiae (St Thomas
   Aquinas), 150, 152
Swift, J., 20

Tacitus, 100, 101
Tancred de Hauteville, 105
Tennyson, 44
Tertullian, 117
The City (Weber), 55
Theodoric, 73, 78
Theodosius I, 53, 65
Thomas Aquinas, St, 54, 150,
   152
Thompson, E. A., 101

Timaeus (Plato), 159
Tocqueville, A. de, 23
Tristan, 122, 124, 127
Tristan and Isolde (Gottfried of
    Strasbourg), 124
Troilus and Criseyde (Chaucer),
    127
Twain, M., 44

Ulfila, 101

Van der Paele, 154
Van Eyck, 154
Vasari, 15

Vico, 21, 22
Villon, 148
Vita Nuova (Dante), 124
Voltaire, 18

Weber, M., 27, 55
Western Economy, Birth of the
    (Latouche), 46
White, T. H., 44
Wife of Bath, 128
William the Conqueror, 106,
    113

Zacharias, 82

MORE ABOUT PENGUINS
AND PELICANS

Penguinews, which appears every month, contains details of all the new books issued by Penguins as they are published. From time to time it is supplemented by *Penguins in Print*, which is a complete list of all books published by Penguins which are in print. (There are well over three thousand of these.)

A specimen copy of *Penguinews* will be sent to you free on request, and you can become a subscriber for the price of the postage. For a year's issues (including the complete lists) please send 4s. if you live in the United Kingdom, or 8s. if you live elsewhere. Just write to Dept EP, Penguin Books Ltd, Harmondsworth, Middlesex, enclosing a cheque or postal order, and your name will be added to the mailing list.

Another Pelican book is described on the following page.

Note: *Penguinews* and *Penguins in Print* are not available in the U.S.A. or Canada

EUROPEAN CULTURE AND OVERSEAS EXPANSION

Carlo M. Cipolla

Why did Europe dominate the world for four centuries after the Renaissance?

In answering one of the crucial 'Why's' of history, Professor Cipolla sees the simultaneous appearance and combination of the cannon and of the sailing-ship, along with clocks, as providing the essential instruments of European expansion, whereby world-wide trade and later seaborne conquest were made possible. To these he adds the growing divergencies between Eastern and Western philosophy during the fifteenth century.

So great was the technological gap between East and West that for centuries European artillery, clocks and lenses were regarded as mere toys for the amusement of the Chinese Emperor. And Europe was left unchecked, to extend her influence overseas.

'Like all his work it is exciting, original, intellectually alive, and deeply researched – and the scholarship is carried with such wit and panache that he is immediately readable' – *Sunday Times*.

'Argues his case brilliantly and undoubtedly provides the correct answer to a fascinating historical problem' – *The Times Literary Supplement*.

Also available

LITERACY AND DEVELOPMENT IN THE WEST
THE ECONOMIC HISTORY OF WORLD POPULATION

Not for sale in the U.S.A.